OH
TRUFFLES
BY
AU CHOCOLAT

OH TRUFFLES BY AU CHOCOLAT

Perfect Recipes
for Every Chocolate Lover's Fantasy

BY
PAM WILLIAMS
and
RITA MORIN

𝔰𝔡

STEIN AND DAY/*Publishers*/New York

First published in the United States of America in 1984
Copyright © 1983 by Wilmor Publishing Corporation
All rights reserved, Stein and Day, Incorporated
Printed in the United States of America

STEIN AND DAY / *Publishers*
Scarborough House
Briarcliff Manor, N.Y. 10510

Library of Congress Cataloging in Publication Data

Williams, Pam.
    Oh truffles by Au chocolat.

    Includes index.
    1. Candy.   2. Cookery (Chocolate)   I. Morin, Rita.
II. Title.
TX 791.W58   1984   641.8′53   84-40234
ISBN 0-8128-6225-2 (pbk.)

Photography by John Sherlock, Vancouver, B.C.

To Rita who made it happen –
may your future be rich with "Black Gold."

Contents

Introduction

Introduction

Since their inception, Truffles have meant the ultimate chocolate experience for generations of chocolate lovers. Infused with liqueur or fruit and nut flavorings, truffle centers let nothing come between the chocolate lover and the chocolate itself. Technically and historically, a Truffle is a combination of chocolate lightened with eggs, butter or cream and then flavored. Developed by a French chef it was originally rolled in cocoa in a free form shape that resembled the black fungus truffle from which it got its name.

During my years of "Truffletiering," I have tested and developed many different combinations of chocolate and flavorings. The results of all that experience are contained in the pages of this book. From the deep dark Espresso Truffle to the soft, melting Bailey's Cream Truffle lies the perfect recipe for the Truffle to fulfill any chocolate lover's fantasy.

Making Truffles is deceptively easy – merely the combining of chocolate with ingredients that lighten and further flavor it. What differentiates the ultimate truffle from a sad replica is the quality of the ingredients that are used.

Start with the finest chocolate you can find. (I've talked about chocolate in greater detail in the last chapter). Then, add to that chocolate the freshest eggs, butter or cream. Use the following recipes as a guide only. I suggest you try all the basic recipes first to find the one recipe that has just the right consistency and flavor to suit your own taste buds. You can then enhance the basic recipe with whatever flavorings you like. I have specified certain combinations of ingredients for each different truffle. My taste buds differ from yours so please feel free to experiment as much as you like. A few points to keep in mind while experimenting are: The higher the proportion of chocolate to other ingredients, the firmer the truffle. Also, the dark chocolate truffles will be firmer than the milk, cream or white truffles and will accept more liquid while still holding a shape.

I've included decorating suggestions for each Truffle. This will give you some guidelines to use while also showing the variety of treatments for the outside of the Truffle. The only point to remember is that a very soft truffle center is best served wrapped in a chocolate coating because at room temperature it may be too soft to pick up.

Different occasions will call for different kinds of decoration on your Truffles. A rough basket filled with cocoa and nut rolled truffles is the perfect ending to a casual summer barbeque. An intimate holiday dinner might need the elegant understatement of a Calvados Truffle decorated to look like a small perfect apple. Whatever the season, Truffles make the ultimate gift of love and appreciation.

Enjoy— and happy Truffletiering!

Pam Williams

The Classic Recipes

This chapter contains the basic Truffle recipes from easy to complicated, from adequate to very, very rich. These are the recipes upon which all other recipes in this book are based. Time, taste and availability of ingredients will determine which one is perfect for a certain occasion.

One very important point to remember, truffles can only be as good as the ingredients from which they are made. The finest quality of chocolate or cocoa and the freshest of cream, butter and eggs will make a considerable difference in the finished product.

We suggest you try all the recipes in this chapter and judge which one you prefer before carrying on to the fabulous variations in the following chapters. Also, note that only simple, basic decorating suggestions are made in this chapter. More elaborate and specific decorations are suggested with added flavourings in the following chapters.

Classic Recipes Index

Cocoa Truffle

Ingredients:

Yield: 24-28

½ cup	125 mL	Cocoa (preferably high quality Dutch process Cocoa)
1-¼ cups	300 mL	Icing Sugar, sifted (also called Confectioner's Sugar)
½ cup	125 mL	Unsalted butter at room temperature
½ cup	125 mL	Cocoa (for decoration)
½ cup	125 mL	Icing Sugar (for decoration)

Preparation:

1. Place all ingredients in an electric mixer.
2. Beat at low speed to blend.
3. Beat at high speed 3 – 5 minutes until light and fluffy.
4. Chill mixture in refrigerator for 1 hour or until firm enough to roll.
5. Scrape spoon or melon-ball cutter across surface of mixture; quickly press with fingertips into 1-inch (2.5 cm) balls. Freeze well wrapped in plastic.

Suggested Decoration:

Roll half of the balls in Cocoa and the other half in Icing Sugar. Place in cups. This type of decoration is as quick as truffles themselves. Serve at room temperature.

Storage:

Store in refrigerator well wrapped in plastic for up to one month. Store in freezer well wrapped in plastic for several months.

Notes:

This is a quick and easy truffle mixture but it will not have the rich taste and texture of chocolate based recipes.

Ganache Truffle

Ingredients:

Yield: 28–32

8 oz	250 g	Chocolate (chopped fine)
⅓ cup	75 mL	Whipping cream
1 lb	500 g	Chocolate (for decoration)

Preparation:

1. Bring cream just to a boil in a heavy saucepan. Remove from heat.
2. Beat chocolate into cream using hand mixer or whisk. Beat until smooth and all chocolate is melted.
3. Chill in refrigerator until firm (approximately 1–3 hours).
4. Scrape spoon or melon-ball cutter across surface of mixture; quickly press with fingertips into 1-inch (2.5 cm) balls. Freeze well wrapped in plastic.

Suggested Decoration:

Dip in same flavor of chocolate as used to make truffles. See dipping instructions in last chapter.

Storage:

Store in refrigerator well wrapped in plastic for 1 week or freeze in plastic wrap for 1–2 months.

Notes:

Try to make sure that your whipping cream is very fresh as it is the only ingredient other than the chocolate and contributes significantly to the final flavor.

Buttery Truffle

Ingredients:

Yield: 40 – 50

8 oz	250 g	Chocolate
½ cup	125 mL	Unsalted butter at room temperature (European style butter preferred)
1 lb	500 g	Chocolate (for decoration)

Preparation:

1. Carefully melt chocolate in a double boiler over hot water. When melted, remove from heat.
2. Vigorously beat butter into warm chocolate with whisk or at high speed with a hand held mixer until light and fluffy. (3 – 5 minutes)
3. Chill until firm (approximately 1 – 3 hours)
4. Scrape spoon or melon-ball cutter across surface of mixture; quickly press with fingertips into 1-inch (2.5 cm) balls. Freeze well wrapped in plastic.

Suggested Decoration:

This is a very soft, buttery truffle that may melt easily. It should be dipped in chocolate. (See instructions in last chapter).

Storage:

Can be stored in the refrigerator well wrapped in plastic for 1 month. Freeze well wrapped in plastic for an indefinite period.

Notes:

All recipes call for unsalted butter. We found the European style of unsalted butter with its slightly "Crème Fraîche" flavor the best. Salted butter can be substituted with a resulting salty taste to the truffles.

Luxurious Truffle

Ingredients:

Yield: 28 – 32

8 oz	250 g	Chocolate
3 tblsp	45 mL	Unsalted butter at room temperature
1 cup	250 mL	Whipping cream

Preparation:

1. Scald cream in heavy saucepan. Remove from heat and let cool to room temperature. Strain through sieve.
2. Melt chocolate in double boiler over hot water. When melted, remove from heat.
3. Beat butter into chocolate until smooth.
4. Vigourously beat cream into chocolate/butter mixture with whisk until light and fluffy.
5. Chill until firm, approximately 1–3 hours.
6. Scrape spoon or melon-ball cutter across surface of mixture; quickly press with fingertips into 1-inch (2.5 cm) balls. Freeze well wrapped in plastic.

Suggested Decoration:

This truffle is firm enough at room temperature to roll in a variety of coatings; nuts, cocoa, sugars, and other crushed confections according to flavorings added.

Storage:

Store tightly wrapped in plastic in refrigerator for 1 week. Freeze up to one month tightly wrapped in plastic.

Notes:

This is a great all purpose recipe that will readily accept any flavorings, except added liquids or liqueurs. If liquids are added, reduce amount of cream by amount of liquid you are adding.

Rich European Truffle

Ingredients:

Yield: 40–50

8 oz	250 g	Chocolate
½ cup	125 mL	Unsalted butter (room temperature
3	3	Egg yolks at room temperature
1 lb	500 g	Chocolate (for decoration)

Preparation:

1. Melt chocolate in double boiler over hot water just until melted. Remove from heat.
2. Vigorously beat butter and egg yolks into chocolate.
3. Chill until firm (approximately 1–3 hours.)
4. Scrape spoon or melon-ball cutter across surface of mixture; quickly press with fingertips into 1-inch (2.5 cm) balls. Freeze well wrapped in plastic.

Suggested Decoration:

These are very rich, soft truffles when at room temperature. They should be dipped in chocolate to retain shape and to keep truffle moist. See instructions for chocolate dipping in last chapter.

Storage:

The egg yolks make these truffles very perishable. They should be refrigerated until 5 to 10 minutes before serving. If they are to be stored, they can be frozen for up to one month tightly wrapped in plastic bags.

Notes:

This rich truffle mixture is the most appropriate for liquor enhanced truffles. The egg yolks not only add a silken texture to the mixture but also help to absorb the added liquor or liquid.

French Truffle

Ingredients:

Yield: 25–30

8 oz	250 g	Chocolate (chopped into small pieces)
⅓ cup	75 mL	Crème Fraîche (see last chapter for directions)
1 tbsp	15 mL	Unsalted butter at room temperature
½ cup	125 mL	Sweetened or unsweetened cocoa for decoration

Preparation:

1. Bring Crème Fraîche to a boil in a heavy saucepan, stirring constantly. Remove from heat.
2. Whisk chocolate into crème until melted and mixture is smooth.
3. Whisk butter into chocolate and crème mixture until smooth.
4. Refrigerate until firm approximately 1–3 hours.
5. Scrape spoon or melon-ball cutter across surface of mixture; quickly press with fingertips into 1-inch (2.5 cm) balls. Freeze well wrapped in plastic.

Suggested Decoration:

Roll each ball in unsweetened or sweetened cocoa to coat. Chill again until firm. Serve from the refrigerator or allow to soften 10 minutes before serving.

Storage:

Store in the refrigerator tightly sealed in plastic for one week. Freeze tightly sealed in plastic for up to 1 month.

Notes:

This truffle with its sweet/sour flavor is best suited for adult palates. Flavor it with liqueur (2 tsp) (10 mL) and you will have the classic French truffle.

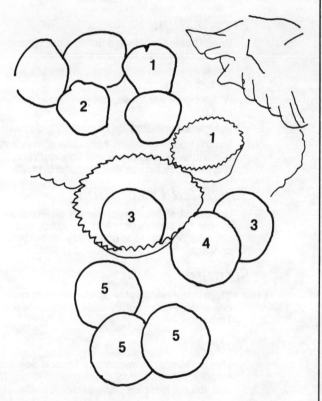

1. White Chocolate Truffle Cream
2. Milk Chocolate Truffle Cream
3. Very Bittersweet Chocolate Truffle
4. Mellow Milk Chocolate Truffle
5. Pure White Chocolate Truffle

For Pure Chocolate Lovers

Truffle recipes using combinations of chocolate, pure chocolate and nothing but chocolate.

Chocolate Truffle Recipe Index

Very Bittersweet Chocolate Truffle

Ingredients:

Yield: 25–30

2 oz	55 g	Unsweetened Chocolate (chopped fine)
6 oz	170 g	Semisweet Chocolate (chopped fine)
⅓ cup	75 mL	Crème Fraîche (see last chapter for instructions)
1 tbsp	15 mL	Unsalted butter at room temperature
½ cup	125 mL	Unsweetened Cocoa (for decoration)

Preparation:

1. Bring crème fraîche to a boil in heavy saucepan stirring constantly. Remove from heat.
2. Whisk both chocolates into crème fraîche until melted and mixture is smooth.
3. Whisk in butter until smooth.
4. Refrigerate until firm, approximately 1–3 hours.
5. Scrape spoon or melon-ball cutter across surface of mixture; quickly press with fingertips into 1-inch (2.5 cm) balls. Freeze well wrapped in plastic.

Suggested Decoration:

Roll each ball into unsweetened cocoa. Chill until firm.

Storage:

Store in refrigerator well wrapped in plastic for one week. Can be frozen well wrapped in plastic for up to one month.

Notes:

This is the creamiest bittersweet truffle in existence. I have always found it to be especially loved by men who traditionally don't like "sweets". If possible, use the same brand of chocolate for both unsweetened and semisweet flavours of chocolate.

Deep Dark Chocolate Truffle

Ingredients:

Yield: 28–32

8 oz	250 g	Semisweet chocolate (chopped fine)
½ cup	125 mL	Whipping Cream
1 lb	500 g	Semisweet chocolate (for decoration)

Preparation:

1. Bring cream just to a boil in a heavy saucepan. Remove from heat.
2. Beat chocolate into cream using hand mixer or whisk. Beat until smooth and all chocolate is melted.
3. Chill in refrigerator until firm. (approximately 1–3 hours).
4. Scrape spoon or melon-ball cutter across surface of mixture; quickly press with fingertips into 1-inch (2.5 cm) balls. Freeze well wrapped in plastic.

Suggested Decoration:

Dip into semisweet chocolate and decorate with lines of the same chocolate across top or swirl top as you hand dip. See instructions in last chapter for dipping instructions.

Storage:

Store in refrigerator well wrapped in plastic for 1 week or freeze in plastic wrap for 1–2 months.

Notes:

This is a dark chocolate lovers dream! Use only the finest of ingredients for the most spectacular results.

Silky Semisweet Truffle

Ingredients:

Yield: 40–50

4 oz	115 g	Semisweet Chocolate
4 oz	115 g	Milk Chocolate
½ cup	125 mL	Unsalted Butter (room temperature)
1 lb	500 g	Semisweet and Milk Chocolate (for decoration)
⅓ cup	75 mL	Sweetened cocoa (for decoration)

Preparation:

1. Carefully melt chocolate in double boiler over hot water just until melted. Remove from heat.
2. Vigorously beat butter into warm chocolate with a whisk or at high speed with a hand held mixer until light and fluffy.
3. Chill mixture until firm (approximately 1–3 hours)
4. Scrape spoon or melon-ball cutter across surface of mixture; quickly press with fingertips into 1-inch (2.5 cm) balls. Freeze well wrapped in plastic.

Suggested Decoration:

Not a truly dark chocolate truffle, it is best dipped in the same proportion milk chocolate to semisweet chocolate to coat. A dusting of sweetened cocoa when truffles are still wet adds a finishing touch. See instructions in last chapter.

Storage:

Well wrapped in plastic it can be kept in the refrigerator for up to 1 month and in the freezer indefinitely.

Notes:

This is a very creamy truffle with a flavor that will satisfy both milk and dark chocolate lovers.

Mellow Milk Chocolate Truffle

Ingredients:

Yield: 32 – 35

8 oz	250 g	Milk Chocolate
½ cup	125 mL	Unsalted Butter (room temperature)
3	3	Egg yolks at room temperature
1 lb	500 g	Milk Chocolate for decoration

Preparation:

1. Melt chocolate in double boiler over hot water just until melted. Remove from heat.
2. Vigorously beat butter and egg yolks into chocolate.
3. Chill until firm. (Approximately 1 – 3 hours).
4. Scrape spoon or melon-ball cutter across surface of mixture; quickly press with fingertips into 1-inch (2.5 cm) balls. Freeze well wrapped in plastic.

Suggested Decoration:

These are very soft, rich truffles when at room temperature, so they should be dipped in chocolate. I prefer to dip milk chocolate truffles in milk chocolate followed with a dusting of milk chocolate shavings while truffles are still wet.

Storage:

Refrigerate well wrapped in plastic for up to one week. Take out of refrigerator only 5 – 10 minutes before serving. They can be frozen well wrapped in plastic for up to 1 month.

Notes:

This truffle is so rich with milk chocolate, it will drive a milk chocolate lover wild! These should be handled with care as milk chocolate can be very soft at room temperature.

Dusty Cream Chocolate Truffle

Ingredients:

Yield: 45 – 50

4 oz	125 g	Milk Chocolate
4 oz	125 g	White Chocolate
2 tbsp	30 mL	Unsalted butter at room temperature
1 cup	250 mL	Whipping cream
1 lb	500 g	Milk or White Chocolate (for decoration)

Preparation:

1. Scald cream in heavy saucepan. Remove from heat and let cool to room temperature. Strain through sieve.
2. Carefully melt both chocolates together in double boiler over hot water. Remove from heat.
3. With a whisk, beat butter into chocolate until smooth.
4. Vigorously beat cream into chocolate/butter mixture with whisk until light and fluffy.
5. Chill until firm, approximately 2 – 4 hours.
6. Scrape spoon or melon-ball cutter across surface of mixture; quickly press with fingertips into 1-inch (2.5cm) balls. Freeze well wrapped in plastic.

Suggested Decoration:

As this is a very soft truffle, it should be dipped in chocolate – either milk or white chocolate would be best. Finish the decorations with stripes of the contrasting chocolate.

Storage:

Store in the refrigerator tightly sealed in plastic for one week. Freeze tightly sealed in plastic for up to one month.

Notes:

This flavour of truffle is the perfect base for delicate nut, café au lait, Bailey's Cream and caramel flavorings.

Pure White Chocolate Truffle

Ingredients:
Yield: 45–50

8 oz	250 g	White Chocolate
2 tbsp	30 mL	Unsalted butter at room temperature
1 cup	250 mL	Whipping cream
1 lb	500 g	White Chocolate (for decoration)

Preparation:
1. Scald cream in heavy saucepan. Remove from heat and let cool to room temperature. Strain through sieve.
2. Melt chocolate in double boiler over hot water. When melted, remove from heat.
3. Beat butter into chocolate until smooth.
4. Vigorously beat cream into chocolate/butter mixture with whisk until light and fluffy.
5. Chill until firm, approximately 1–3 hours.
6. Scrape spoon or melon-ball cutter across surface of mixture; quickly press with fingertips into 1-inch (2.5 cm) balls. Freeze well wrapped in plastic.

Suggested Decoration:
White chocolate on white chocolate makes this a "pure" white chocolate truffle! Sprinkle with shaved white chocolate while the truffle is still wet. Or, simply roll the white truffle in colored sugar for a festive look.

Storage:
Store tightly wrapped in plastic in refrigerator for 1 week. Freeze up to one month tightly wrapped in plastic.

Notes:
The *only* truffle for white chocolate lovers!

Truffle Cream

Ingredients:
Yield: 60

8 oz	250 g	Chocolate (any flavor)
½ cup	125 mL	Unsalted butter (room temperature)
1 tsp	5 mL	Choice of flavoring (optional)
5 dozen	5 dozen	Small candy cups

Preparation:
1. Carefully melt chocolate in a double boiler over hot water. When melted, remove from heat.
2. Vigorously beat butter and flavorings into warm chocolate with whisk or at high speed with a hand held mixer until very light and fluffy. Mixture should hold a peak when beater is removed.
3. Spoon mixture into a pastry bag fitted with a star tip.
4. Pipe into candy cups. Refrigerate cups as soon as possible as they can melt in a warm room.

Storage:
Can be stored in the refrigerator well wrapped in plastic for 1 month. Freeze well wrapped in plastic for an indefinite period.

Notes:
Truffle Cream is a very easy after dinner chocolate you can make ahead of time and have frozen ready to serve.

Notes

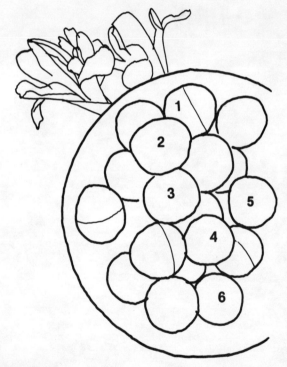

1. Coconut Truffle
2. Meringue Truffle
3. Peppermint Truffle
4. Cherry Truffle
5. Mocha Truffle
6. Chocolate Chip Truffle

Flavor Me Fantastic

Luscious truffle recipes combining chocolate with flavorings such as extracts, oils, fruit juices, fruit and dessert chunks.

Flavor Me Fantastic Recipe Index

Espresso Truffle

Ingredients:

Yield 30–35

2 oz	55 g	Unsweetened Chocolate (chopped fine)
6 oz	170 g	Semisweet Chocolate (chopped fine)
⅓ cup	75 mL	Crème fraîche (see last chapter for instructions)
1 tbsp	15 mL	Unsalted butter at room temperature
1 tsp	125 mL	Instant Espresso
½ cup	125 mL	Espresso Beans
1 lb	500 g	Bittersweet Chocolate for decoration
¼ cup	50 mL	Espresso Beans for decoration

Preparation:

1. Bring crème fraîche to a boil in heavy saucepan stirring constantly. Remove from heat and add instant espresso.
2. Whisk both chocolates into crème fraîche until melted and mixture is smooth.
3. Whisk in butter until smooth. Fold in Espresso Beans.
4. Refrigerate until firm, approximately 1–3 hours.
5. Scrape spoon or melon-ball cutter across surface of mixture; quickly press with fingertips into 1-inch (2.5 cm) balls. Freeze well wrapped in plastic.

Suggested Decoration:

Dip in Bittersweet chocolate and place two Espresso Beans on top of each truffle while chocolate is still wet.

Storage:

Store in refrigerator well wrapped in plastic for one week. Can be frozen well wrapped in plastic for up to one month.

Notes:

A fabulous crunchy end to the perfect meal. Allow no more than 2 per person as there is a high level of caffeine in each truffle.

Peppermint Truffle

Ingredients:

Yield: 28 – 32

4 oz	115 g	Semisweet Chocolate
4 oz	115 g	Milk Chocolate
½ cup	125 mL	Unsalted Butter (room temperature)
1 tsp	5 mL	Peppermint Extract or oil
½ cup	125 mL	Ground Peppermints (optional)
1 lb	500 g	Semisweet Chocolate (for decoration)
¼ lb	115 g	Green confectioners coating (for decoration)

Preparation:

1. Carefully melt chocolate in double boiler over hot water just until melted. Remove from heat.
2. Add peppermint extract or oil mixing well.
3. Vigorously beat butter into warm chocolate with a whisk or at high speed with a hand held mixer until light and fluffy.
4. Fold in ground peppermints if desired.
5. Chill mixture until firm (approximately 1 – 3 hours).
6. Scrape spoon or melon-ball cutter across surface of mixture; quickly press with fingertips into 1-inch (2.5 cm) balls. Freeze well wrapped in plastic.

Suggested Decoration:

With any mint truffle, I always prefer green stripes on a semisweet dipped truffle. (See instructions in last chapter). If you want the crunchiness of ground peppermint you can also reserve a small amount and sprinkle on top of the truffle while the chocolate is still wet.

Storage:

Can be kept in the refrigerator well wrapped in plastic for up to 1 month and in the freezer indefinitely.

Notes:

I love just a hint of mint so I add extract or oil only until I can taste it as an aftertaste rather than as a distinct taste or flavor.

Orange Truffle

Ingredients:

Yield: 44 – 48

8 oz	250 g	Semisweet Chocolate
½ cup	125 mL	Unsalted Butter (room temperature)
½ cup	125 mL	Marmalade
1½ cups	375 mL	Candied orange peel (for decorating). See last chapter for instructions

Preparation:

1. Carefully melt chocolate in a double boiler over hot water. When melted, remove from heat.
2. Beat butter into warm chocolate with a whisk or at high speed with a hand held mixer until light and fluffy (3 – 5 minutes).
3. Fold marmalade into truffle mixture mixing thoroughly.
4. Chill until firm (approx. 1 – 3 hours)
5. Scrape spoon or melon-ball cutter across surface of mixture; quickly press with fingertips into 1-inch (2.5 cm) balls.

Suggested Decoration:

Place chopped candied peel in cake or pie pan. Roll each truffle in peel to cover completely. Place on parchment to set and refrigerate. Truffles must be slightly soft for rolling so peel will stick.

Storage:

Can be stored in the refrigerator well wrapped in plastic for 1 month. Freeze well wrapped in plastic for an indefinite period.

Notes:

These truffles not only taste wonderful but they have a very elegant presentation. If possible, make your own fresh candied peel.

Cherry Truffle

Ingredients:

Yield: 25 – 30

8 oz	250 g	White Chocolate (chopped into small pieces)
⅓ cup	75 mL	Crème Fraîche (see last chapter for directions)
1 tbsp	15 mL	Unsalted butter at room temperature
2 tsp	10 mL	Maraschino or natural cherry juice
few drops	few drops	Red food coloring
1 lb	500 g	Semisweet or Bittersweet Chocolate for decorating
¼ lb	115 g	Light pink confectioners coating (see last chapter for information)

Preparation:

1. Bring Crème Fraîche to a boil in a heavy saucepan stirring constantly. Remove from heat.
2. Whisk chocolate into crème until melted and mixture is smooth.
3. Whisk butter into chocolate and crème mixture until smooth.
4. Whisk in cherry juice, then red food coloring drop by drop until desired color is reached.
5. Refrigerate until firm, approximately 1 – 3 hours.
6. Scrape spoon or melon-ball cutter across surface of mixture; quickly press with fingertips into 1-inch (2.5 cm) balls. Freeze well wrapped in plastic.

Suggested Decoration:

Dip the truffles in Semisweet or Bittersweet chocolate. Use confectioners coating for pink stripes decorating the top. To achieve pale pink stripes, mix ½ white coating with ½ pink coating. (See last chapter for instructions.)

Storage:

Store in the refrigerator tightly sealed in plastic for one week. Freeze tightly sealed in plastic for up to one month.

Notes:

I like these very pale pink on the inside of their almost black shell. They are a sweet truffle with the white chocolate which is why I prefer the dark chocolate coating.

Cafe au Lait Truffle

Ingredients:

Yield: 40 – 45

4 oz	125 g	Milk Chocolate
4 oz	125 g	White Chocolate
2 tbsp	30 mL	Unsalted butter (room temperature)
1 cup	250 mL	Whipping cream
1 tbsp	15 mL	Instant coffee
1 lb	500 g	White or Milk Chocolate for dipping
1 tbsp	15 mL	Cocoa for decoration

Preparation:

1. Scald cream in heavy saucepan. Remove from heat and let cool to room temperature. Strain through sieve.
2. Add instant coffee to scalded cream. Stir to mix.
3. Carefully melt both chocolates together in a double boiler over hot water. Remove from heat.
4. With a whisk, beat butter into chocolate until smooth.
5. Vigorously beat cream/coffee mixture into chocolate/butter mixture until light and fluffy.
6. Chill until firm, approximately 2 – 4 hours.
7. Scrape spoon or melon-ball cutter across surface of mixture; quickly press with fingertrips into 1-inch (2.5 cm) balls. Freeze well wrapped in plastic.

Suggested Decoration:

Dip this truffle in melted white or milk chocolate and dust with cocoa while chocolate is still wet.

Storage:

Store in the refrigerator tightly sealed in plastic for one week. Freeze tightly sealed in plastic for up to one month.

Notes:

This truffle will remind you of that wonderful leisurely morning coffee. Best served as the dessert with fruit or cheese board as it is very rich.

Caramel Truffle

Ingredients:

Yield: 40 – 45

8 oz	250 g	Milk Chocolate
½ cup	125 mL	Unsalted butter at room temperature
½ cup	125 mL	Caramel Sauce
2 cups	500 mL	Caramel sprinkles (for decoration) (See last chapter for instructions)

Preparation:

1. Carefully melt chocolate in a double boiler over hot water. When melted, remove from heat.
2. Beat in the Caramel Sauce until well mixed.
3. Beat butter into warm chocolate with a whisk or at high speed with a hand mixer until light and fluffy. (3 – 5 minutes).
4. Chill until firm, approximately 1 – 3 hours.
5. Scrape spoon or melon-ball cutter across surface of mixture; quickly press with fingertips into 1-inch (2.5 cm) balls. Freeze well wrapped in plastic.

Suggested Decoration:

Even though this truffle is very soft, it can be rolled in caramel sprinkles but should be done on the day you plan to serve them. The caramel sprinkles will get sticky if left out.

Storage:

Store tightly wrapped in plastic in refrigerator for 1 week. Freeze up to one month tightly wrapped in plastic.

Notes:

I love using the caramel sprinkles to coat these truffles as they impart a glistening sparkle to any dessert tray.

Ginger Truffle

Ingredients:

Yield: 30 – 35

2 oz	55 g	Unsweetened Chocolate (chopped fine)
6 oz	170 g	Semisweet Chocolate (chopped fine)
⅓ cup	75 mL	Crème Fraîche (see last chapter for instructions)
1 tbsp	15 mL	Unsalted butter at room temperature
½ cup	125 mL	Chopped ginger
⅓ cup	75 mL	Ginger slivered for decoration
1 lb	500 g	Bittersweet chocolate for decoration

Preparation:

1. Bring Crème Fraîche to a boil in heavy saucepan stirring constantly. Remove from heat.
2. Whisk both chocolates into Crème Fraîche until melted and mixture is smooth.
3. Whisk in butter until smooth.
4. Fold in chopped ginger.
5. Refrigerate until firm, approximately 1 – 3 hours.
6. Scrape spoon or melon-ball cutter across surface of mixture; quickly press with fingertips into 1-inch (2.5 cm) balls. Freeze well wrapped in plastic.

Suggested Decoration:

Dip each truffle in melted bittersweet chocolate and decorate each with slivered ginger while chocolate is still wet.

Storage:

Store in the refrigerator well wrapped in plastic for one week. Can be frozen well wrapped in plastic for up to one month.

Notes:

I've found that most ginger lovers like a bittersweet chocolate but you can substitute any flavor of chocolate that you like.

Vanilla Truffle

Ingredients:

Yield: 45 – 50

4 oz	125 g	Milk Chocolate
4 oz	125 g	White Chocolate
2 tbsp	30 mL	Unsalted Butter at room temperature
1 cup	250 mL	Whipping Cream
1	1	Vanilla Bean
¼ cup	50 mL	Cocoa for decoration
¼ cup	50 mL	Icing Sugar for decoration

Preparation:

1. Add vanilla bean to Cream. Scald cream, remove from heat and let cool to room temperature. Remove vanilla bean and strain cream through sieve. Split the vanilla bean lengthwise, scrape out seeds and stir into cream. Discard vanilla bean.
2. Carefully melt both chocolates together in double boiler over hot water. Remove from heat.
3. With a whisk, beat butter into chocolate until smooth.
4. Vigorously beat cream into chocolate/butter mixture with whisk until light and fluffy.
5. Chill until firm, approximately 2 – 4 hours.
6. Scrape spoon or melon-ball cutter across surface of mixture; quickly press with fingertips into 1-inch (2.5 cm) balls. Freeze well wrapped in plastic.

Suggested Decoration:

Roll truffles in a combination of cocoa and icing sugar that has been thoroughly mixed. Refrigerate truffles immediately.

Storage:

Store in the refrigerator tightly sealed in plastic for one week. Freeze tightly sealed in plastic for up to one month.

Notes:

The wonderful aroma and taste of vanilla permeates this truffle. A treat for all vanilla lovers.

Coconut Truffle

Ingredients:

Yield: 40 – 45

8 oz	250 g	White Chocolate
2 tbsp	30 mL	Unsalted butter at room temperature
1 cup	250 mL	Whipping cream
½ cup	125 mL	Fine shredded coconut (fresh if possible)
1 lb	500 g	Semisweet chocolate (for decoration)
1 lb	500 g	White chocolate (for decoration)

Preparation:

1. Mix coconut with cream in a heavy saucepan.
2. Scald cream and coconut. Remove from heat and let cool to room temperature.
3. Melt chocolate in double boiler over hot water. When melted, remove from heat.
4. Beat butter into chocolate until smooth.
5. Vigorously beat the cream and coconut mixture into the chocolate/butter mixture with a whisk until light and fluffy.
6. Chill until firm, approximately 1 – 3 hours.
7. Scrape spoon or melon-ball cutter across surface of mixture; quickly press with fingertips into 1-inch (2.5 cm) balls. Freeze well wrapped in plastic.

Suggested Decoration:

Dip coconut truffles in semisweet chocolate covering completely. Let chocolate cool and set. Dip ½ of each truffle in white chocolate to coat over the semisweet chocolate layer.

Storage:

Store tightly wrapped in plastic in refrigerator for 1 week. Freeze up to one month tightly wrapped in plastic.

Notes:

This is one of my favorite ways of decorating truffles. It makes them a little fatter but very elegant. Just be careful to clean your fingers between each dipping in white chocolate so no finger prints appear on the semisweet layer.

Strawberry Truffle

Ingredients:

Yield: 42 – 45

8 oz	250 g	Milk Chocolate
½ cup	125 mL	Unsalted Butter (room temperature)
3	3	Egg yolks at room temperature
½ cup	125 mL	Strawberry Preserves
2 cups	500 mL	Pink colored sugar (for decoration)

Preparation:

1. Melt chocolate in double boiler over hot water just until melted. Remove from heat.
2. Vigorously beat butter and egg yolks into chocolate.
3. Gently fold in strawberry preserves, mixing thoroughly.
4. Chill until firm. (Approximately 1 – 3 hours).
5. Scrape spoon or melon-ball cutter across surface of mixture; quickly press with fingertips into 1-inch (2.5 cm) balls. Freeze well wrapped in plastic.

Suggested Decoration:

Lightly dip truffles in pink colored sugar. Chill until firm.

Storage:

Refrigerate well wrapped in plastic for up to one week. Take out of refrigerator only 5 – 10 minutes before serving. They can be frozen well wrapped in plastic for up to 1 month.

Notes:

Everyone is crazy about strawberries and chocolate. This truffle combines both flavors for an anytime of the year strawberry feast.

Mocha Truffle

Ingredients:

Yield: 32 – 35

8 oz	250 g	Milk Chocolate
½ cup	125 mL	Unsalted Butter (room temperature)
3	3	Egg yolks at room temperature
1 tbsp	15 mL	Instant Coffee
1 lb	500 g	Semisweet Chocolate (for decoration)
¼ lb	115 g	Milk Chocolate (for decoration)

Preparation:

1. Melt chocolate in double boiler over hot water just until melted. Remove from heat.
2. Stir instant coffee into melted chocolate and mix until dissolved.
3. Vigorously beat butter and egg yolks into chocolate.
4. Chill until firm. (Approximately 1 – 3 hours).
5. Scrape spoon or melon-ball cutter across surface of mixture; quickly press with fingertips into 1-inch (2.5 cm) balls. Freeze well wrapped in plastic.

Suggested Decoration:

Dip in semisweet chocolate coating completely. Decorate top with milk chocolate stripes. See instructions in last Chapter.

Storage:

Refrigerate well wrapped in plastic for up to one week. Take out of refrigerator only 5 – 10 minutes before serving. They can be frozen well wrapped in plastic for up to 1 month.

Notes:

The smooth mellow coffee flavor makes this truffle an all around hit.

Raspberry Truffle

Ingredients:

Yield: 43 – 45

8 oz	250 g	Semisweet Chocolate
½ cup	125 mL	Unsalted butter at room temperature
3	3	Egg yolks at room temperature
½ cup	125 mL	Seedless Raspberry jelly
1 lb	500 g	White Chocolate (for decoration)
1 lb	500 g	Fresh Raspberries if available OR
¼ cup	50 mL	Red colored sugar

Preparation:

1. Melt chocolate in double boiler over hot water just until melted. Remove from heat.
2. Vigorously beat butter and egg yolks into chocolate.
3. Fold in Raspberry Jelly just until it forms ribbons of color throughout the chocolate.
4. Chill until firm, approximately 1 – 3 hours.
5. Scrape spoon or melon-ball cutter across surface of mixture; quickly press with fingertips into 1-inch (2.5 cm) balls. Freeze well wrapped in plastic.
6. Cut fresh Raspberries (if using) in half and dry on paper towels.

Suggested Decoration:

Dip truffle carefully in white chocolate coating truffle completely. Place ½ raspberry into chocolate on top of truffle while chocolate is still wet. If fresh raspberries are not available, sprinkle top with red colored sugar while chocolate is still wet.

Storage:

The egg yolks make these truffles very perishable. They should be refrigerated until 5 – 10 minutes before serving. They can be frozen for up to one month tightly wrapped in plastic.

Notes:

The surprise of raspberries and dark chocolate inside the beautifully finished outside make this truffle outstanding. If using fresh raspberries, decorate them the day they are to be served.

Lemon Truffle

Ingredients:

Yield: 40 – 45

8 oz	250 g	White Chocolate
2 tbsp	30 mL	Unsalted Butter at room temperature
1 cup	250 mL	Whipping Cream
¼ cup	50 mL	Finely chopped lemon zest (see instructions in last chapter)
¼ cup	50 mL	Slivered lemon zest (for decoration)
1 lb	500 g	White chocolate (for decoration)

Preparation:

1. Mix ¼ cup (50 mL) chopped lemon zest in heavy saucepan with cream.
2. Scald cream and lemon zest. Remove from heat and let cool to room temperature.
3. Melt chocolate in double boiler over hot water. When melted, remove from heat.
4. Beat butter into chocolate until smooth.
5. Vigorously beat the cream/lemon zest mixture into the chocolate/butter mixture with a whisk until light and fluffy.
6. Chill until firm, approximately 1 – 3 hours.
7. Scrape spoon or melon-ball cutter across surface of mixture; quickly press with fingertips into 1-inch (2.5 cm) balls. Freeze well wrapped in plastic.

Suggested Decoration:

Dip truffles in white chocolate and decorate with slivered lemon zest while chocolate is still wet.

Storage:

Store tightly wrapped in plastic in refrigerator for 1 week. Freeze up to one month tightly wrapped in plastic.

Notes:

This truffle can also be done substituting bittersweet chocolate for those dark chocolate and fruit lovers.

Pineapple Truffle

Ingredients: Yield: 45 – 50

8 oz	250 g	Milk Chocolate
½ cup	125 mL	Unsalted butter at room temperature
3	3	Egg yolks at room temperature
1 can	1 can	Pineapple chunks drained and dried on paper towels
1 lb	500 g	Milk Chocolate for decoration
¼ cup	50 mL	Yellow Sugar

Preparation:

1. Melt chocolate in double boiler over hot water just until melted. Remove from heat.
2. Vigorously beat butter and egg yolks into chocolate.
3. Chill until firm, approximately 1 – 3 hours.
4. Roll into 1-inch (2.5 cm) size balls pressing a chunk of pineapple into center of truffle. Freeze well wrapped in plastic.

Suggested Decoration:

Dip in Milk Chocolate and sprinkle yellow sugar on top while chocolate is still wet.

Storage:

Refrigerate well wrapped in plastic for up to one week. Take out of refrigerator only 5 – 10 minutes before serving. They can be frozen well wrapped in plastic for only up to 1 month.

Notes:

The same procedure can easily be adapted for any dried or candied fruit.

Chocolate Chip Truffle

Ingredients:

Yield: 35–40

8 oz	250 g	Milk Chocolate
½ cup	125 mL	Unsalted Butter at room temperature
3	3	Egg yolks at room temperature
½ cup	125 mL	Tiny chocolate chips
1 lb	500 g	Semisweet chocolate (for decoration

Preparation:

1. Melt chocolate in double boiler over hot water just until melted. Remove from heat.
2. Vigorously beat butter and egg yolks into chocolate.
3. Allow mixture to come to room temperature before folding in chocolate chips mixing well.
4. Chill until firm, approximately 1–3 hours.
5. Scrape spoon or melon-ball cutter across surface of mixture; quickly press with fingertips into 1-inch (2.5 cm) balls. Freeze well wrapped in plastic.

Suggested Decoration:

Dip in semisweet chocolate. The fun is all inside this truffle so we left it plain on the outside.

Storage:

Refrigerate well wrapped in plastic for up to one week. Take out of the refrigerator only 5–10 minutes before serving. They can be frozen well wrapped in plastic for only up to 1 month.

Notes:

Any kind of chocolate chips, butterscotch chips or peanut chips can be substituted for the small tiny ones specified in the recipe.

Meringue Truffle

Ingredients:

Yield: 35 – 40

4 oz	115 g	Semisweet Chocolate
4 oz	115 g	Milk Chocolate
½ cup	125 mL	Unsalted Butter at room temperature.
½ cup	125 mL	Baked crispy meringue chopped in small chunks (see instructions in last chapter)
1 lb	500 g	Semisweet chocolate (for decoration)
¼ lb	115 g	Milk chocolate (for decoration)

Preparation:

1. Carefully melt chocolate in double boiler over hot water. When melted, remove from heat.
2. Vigorously beat butter into warm chocolate with a whisk or at high speed with a hand held mixer until light and fluffy.
3. Fold meringue chunks into chocolate mixture mixing well.
4. Chill mixture until firm, approximately 1-3 hours.
5. Scrape spoon or melon-ball cutter across surface of mixture; quickly press with fingertips into 1-inch (2.5 cm) balls. Freeze well wrapped in plastic.

Suggested Decoration:

Dip truffles in semisweet chocolate to cover. When dry, pipe decoration on the top. (We use a stylized "M" when we make them.)

Storage:

Well wrapped in plastic, can be kept in the refrigerator for up to 1 month and in the freezer indefinitely.

Notes:

A very crispy truffle inside reminiscent of the old fashioned candy bars.

Chocolate Marble Truffle

Ingredients:

Yield: 32 – 35

4 oz	115 g	Semisweet Chocolate
4 oz	115 g	White Chocolate
½ cup	125 mL	Unsalted Butter (room temperature)
3	3	Egg yolks at room temperature
1 lb	500 g	Semisweet Chocolate (for decoration)
¼ cup	50 mL	White Chocolate shavings (for decoration)

Preparation:

1. Melt each chocolate separately in a double boiler over hot water. Remove from heat.
2. Vigorously whisk in 2 egg yolks and ¼ cup (50 mL) butter into semisweet chocolate. Set aside.
3. Vigorously whisk in 1 egg yolk and ¼ cup (50 mL) butter into white chocolate.
4. Carefully spoon white chocolate mixture onto semi-sweet chocolate mixture in 4 piles. Swirl white chocolate through dark mixture with knife.
5. Let chill until firm, (approximately 1 – 3 hours).
6. Scrape spoon or melon-ball cutter across surface of mixture; quickly press with fingertips into 1-inch (2.5 cm) balls. Freeze well wrapped in plastic.

Suggested Decoration:

Dip truffles in melted semisweet chocolate and sprinkle with white chocolate shavings while chocolate is still wet.

Storage:

The egg yolks make these truffles very perishable. They should be refrigerated until 5 – 10 minutes before serving. They can be frozen for up to one month tightly wrapped in plastic bags.

Notes:

This is a gorgeous truffle that brings lots of oohs and ahhs for its presentation as well as its taste.

Black Forest Truffle

Ingredients:

Yield: 30 – 35

2 oz	55 g	Unsweetened Chocolate (chopped fine)
6 oz	170 g	Semisweet Chocolate (chopped fine)
⅓ cup	75 mL	Crème Fraîche (see last chapter for instructions)
1 tbsp	15 mL	Unsalted butter at room temperature
½ cup	125 mL	Chopped Maraschino cherries or any preserved cherries well drained
¼ cup	50 mL	Maraschino cherries slivered for decoration
1 lb	500 g	Semisweet chocolate for decoration

Preparation:

1. Bring Crème Fraîche to a boil in heavy saucepan stirring constantly. Remove from heat.
2. Whisk both chocolates into Crème Fraîche until melted and mixture is smooth.
3. Whisk in butter until mixture is smooth.
4. Fold in chopped cherries until well mixed.
5. Refrigerate until firm, approximately 1-3 hours.
6. Scrape spoon or melon-ball cutter across surface of mixture; quickly press with fingertips into 1-inch (2.5 cm) balls. Freeze well wrapped in plastic.

Suggested Decoration:

Dip each truffle in melted semisweet chocolate and decorate with a slivered cherry on top of each.

Storage:

Store in the refrigerator well wrapped in plastic for one week. Can be frozen well wrapped in plastic for up to one month.

Notes:

Devotees of Black Forest Cakes will love this combination of cherries and chocolate.

Crunchy Caramel Truffle

Ingredients:

Yield: 42 – 45

8 oz	250 g	Milk Chocolate
½ cup	125 mL	Unsalted Butter at room temperature
3	3	Egg yolks at room temperature
¾ cup	175 mL	Caramel sprinkles (see instructions in last chapter)
1 lb	500 g	Milk chocolate (for decoration)
¼ cup	50 mL	Caramel sprinkles (for decoration)

Preparation:

1. Melt chocolate in double boiler over hot water just until melted. Remove from heat.
2. Vigorously beat butter and egg yolks into chocolate.
3. Fold in caramel sprinkles mixing well.
4. Chill until firm – approximately 1–3 hours.
5. Scrape spoon or melon-ball cutter across surface of mixture; quickly press with fingertips into 1-inch (2.5 cm) balls. Freeze well wrapped in plastic.

Suggested Decoration:

Dip in Milk Chocolate to coat and sprinkle with caramel sprinkles while chocolate is still wet.

Storage:

Refrigerate well wrapped in plastic for up to one week. Take out of the refrigerator only 5–10 minutes before serving. They can be frozen well wrapped in plastic for up to 1 month.

Notes:

The smooth mellow milk chocolate is a perfect background for the crunchy caramel.

PearTruffle

Ingredients:

Yield: 30 – 35

8 oz	250 g	Semisweet Chocolate (chopped into small pieces)
½ cup	125 mL	Whipping Cream
½ cup	125 mL	Dried pears, slivered
1 lb	500 g	Semisweet chocolate for decoration
¼ cup	50 mL	Slivered dried pears for decoration

Preparation:

1. Bring cream just to a boil in a heavy saucepan. Remove from heat.
2. Beat chocolate into cream using hand mixer or whisk. Beat until smooth and all chocolate is melted.
3. Add dried pears, mixing well.
4. Chill until firm, approximately 1 – 3 hours.
5. Scrape spoon or melon-ball cutter across surface of mixture; quickly press with fingertips into 1-inch (2.5 cm) balls. Freeze well wrapped in plastic.

Suggested Decoration:

Dip truffle centres in semisweet chocolate to coat. Decorate with slivered pear.

Storage:

Store in refrigerator well wrapped in plastic for 1 week or freeze in plastic wrap for 1 – 2 months.

Notes:

A very elegant truffle that works well with dried apricots as well as pears.

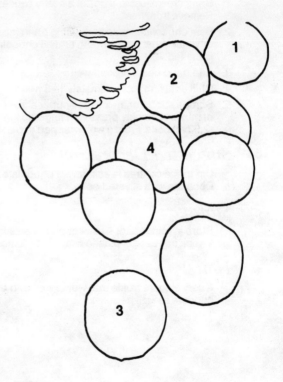

1. Pistachio Truffle
2. Macadamia Nut Truffle
3. Praline Truffle
4. Hazelnut Truffle

Nutty Variations

The classic combination of chocolate and nuts is always a welcome addition to a dessert tray. Each nut flavor needs to be enhanced with just the right type of chocolate for the perfect truffle.

Nutty Variations Recipe Index

Burnt Almond Truffle

Ingredients:

Yield: 30–35

2 oz	55 g	Unsweetened Chocolate (chopped fine)
6 oz	170 g	Semisweet Chocolate (chopped fine)
⅓ cup	75 mL	Crème Fraîche (see last chapter for instructions)
1 tbsp	15 mL	Unsalted Butter at room temperature
½ cup	125 mL	Chopped Toasted Almonds
12 oz	370 g	Semisweet Chocolate for decoration
4 oz	115 g	Unsweetened Chocolate for decoration
½ cup	125 mL	Slivered Toasted Almonds for decoration

Preparation:

1. Bring Crème Fraîche to a boil in a heavy saucepan stirring constantly. Remove from heat.
2. Whisk both chocolates into Crème Fraîche until melted and mixture is smooth.
3. Whisk in butter until smooth.
4. Fold in toasted almonds mixing well.
5. Refrigerate until firm, approximately 1–3 hours.
6. Scrape spoon or melon-ball cutter across surface of mixture; quickly press with fingertips into 1-inch (2.5 cm) balls. Freeze well wrapped in plastic.

Suggested Decoration:

Dip each truffle in a combination of melted unsweetened and semisweet chocolate. Place two or three slivered almonds on top as decoration while chocolate is still wet.

Storage:

Store in the refrigerator well wrapped in plastic for one week. Can be frozen well wrapped in plastic for up to one month.

Notes:

A beautiful bittersweet truffle for the burnt almond lovers in your crowd.

Chestnut Truffle

Ingredients:

Yield: 45 – 50

4 oz	115 g	Semisweet Chocolate
4 oz	115 g	Milk Chocolate
½ cup	125 mL	Unsalted Butter (room temperature)
6	6	Chestnuts, chopped
3 tbsp	45 mL	Chestnut Syrup from can
1 lb	500 g	Semisweet Chocolate for decoration
¼ cup	50 mL	Unsweetened Cocoa

Preparation:

1. Carefully melt chocolate in double boiler over hot water. When melted, remove from heat.
2. Vigorously beat butter into warm chocolate with a whisk or at high speed with a hand held mixer until light and fluffy.
3. Beat in the Chestnut syrup until well mixed.
4. Carefully fold in chopped chestnuts.
5. Chill mixture until firm (approximately 1 – 3 hours).
6. Scrape spoon or melon-ball cutter across surface of mixture; quickly press with fingertips into 1-inch (2.5 cm) balls. Freeze well wrapped in plastic.

Suggested Decoration:

Dip in semisweet chocolate, dusting with cocoa while chocolate is still wet.

Storage:

Well wrapped in plastic can be kept in the refrigerator for up to 1 month and in the freezer indefinitely.

Notes:

Rich chestnut flavor permeates this truffle making it a wonderful addition during winter holidays.

Marzipan Truffle

Ingredients:

Yield: 32-35

8 oz	250 g	Milk Chocolate
½ cup	125 mL	Unsalted Butter at room temperature
3	3	Egg yolks at room temperature
1 cup	250 mL	Marzipan Paste for decoration
¼ cup	50 mL	Sweetened Cocoa for decoration

Preparation:

1. Melt chocolate in double boiler over hot water just until melted. Remove from heat.
2. Vigorously beat butter and egg yolks into chocolate.
3. Chill until firm (approximately 1-3 hours.)
4. Scrape spoon or melon-ball cutter across surface of mixture; quickly press with fingertips into 1-inch (2.5 cm) balls. Freeze well wrapped in plastic.

Suggested Decoration:

Roll Marzipan paste as thin as possible and cut it into 2 inch (5 cm) squares. Place truffle center on square and fold Marzipan around center to cover. Roll between palms until smooth round shape is formed. Dust with sweetened cocoa.

Storage:

Refrigerate well wrapped in plastic for up to one week. They can be frozen well wrapped in plastic for up to one month.

Notes:

The surprise of milk chocolate truffle with the Marzipan cover makes this a truly unique confection.

Golden Almond Truffle

Ingredients:

Yield: 45 – 50

8 oz	250 g	Milk Chocolate
½ cup	125 mL	Unsalted Butter at room temperature
3	3	Egg yolks at room temperature
1 cup	250 mL	Whole Toasted Almonds
1 lb	500 g	Milk Chocolate for decoration

Preparation:

1. Melt chocolate in double boiler over hot water just until melted. Remove from heat.
2. Vigorously beat butter and egg yolks into chocolate.
3. Chill until firm, approximately 1 – 3 hours.
4. Press approximately 1 tbsp. (15 mL) truffle mixture around each almond to form a ball.
5. Freeze well wrapped in plastic.

Suggested Decoration:

Dip in Milk Chocolate, decorating as desired in Milk Chocolate as well.

Storage:

Refrigerate well wrapped in plastic for up to one week. Take out of refrigerator only 5 – 10 minutes before serving. They can be frozen well wrapped in plastic for only up to 1 month.

Notes:

Always a perfect combination – Milk Chocolate and Almonds. A childhood confection for grown up tastes.

Praline Truffle

Ingredients:

Yield: 40 – 45

4 oz	115 g	Semisweet Chocolate
4 oz	115 g	Milk Chocolate
½ cup	125 mL	Unsalted Butter (room temperature)
2 cups	500 mL	Praline chopped coarse (see last chapter for instructions)

Preparation:

1. Carefully melt chocolate in double boiler over hot water. When melted, remove from heat.

2. Vigorously beat butter into warm chocolate with a whisk or at high speed with a hand held mixer until light and fluffy.

3. Chill mixture until firm (approximately 1 – 3 hours).

4. Scrape spoon or melon-ball cutter across surface of mixture; quickly press with fingertips into 1-inch (2.5 cm) balls. Freeze well wrapped in plastic.

Suggested Decoration:

Remove truffle centres from freezer a few at a time and let soften to room temperature. Pour praline onto cookie sheet and roll softened truffle in praline to coat completely. Set in refrigerator briefly to harden. Serve immediately.

Storage:

Without decoration, can be kept in the refrigerator well wrapped in plastic for up to 1 month and in the freezer indefinitely.

Notes:

This is a beautiful glistening truffle but can be decorated only at the last minute as the praline mixture gets very sticky if left out – especially in rainy weather!

Cashew Truffle

Ingredients:
Yield: 35 – 40

2 cups	500 mL	Fresh Roasted Cashews unsalted. (If salted, briefly run under warm water).
8 oz	250 g	Milk Chocolate
1 lb	500 g	Milk Chocolate for decoration
½ cup	125 mL	Cashew Halves

Preparation:
1. Process cashews in blender or food processor until a consistency of chunky butter is reached.
2. Melt chocolate over hot water in double boiler.
3. Beat cashew butter into milk chocolate until well mixed.
4. Chill in refrigerator, approximately 1 hour.
5. Scrape spoon or melon-ball cutter across surface of mixture; quickly press with fingertips into 1-inch (2.5 cm) balls. Freeze well wrapped in plastic.

Suggested Decoration:
Dip truffles centers in melted milk chocolate placing cashew half on top while chocolate is still wet.

Storage:
Can be stored in the refrigerator well wrapped in plastic for 1 month. Freeze well wrapped in plastic for an indefinite period.

Notes:
Cashews and chocolate – heaven!

Peanut Butter Truffle

Ingredients:

Yield: 45–50

8 oz	250 g	White Chocolate
2 tbsp	30 mL	Unsalted Butter at room temperature
1 cup	250 mL	Whipping Cream
1 cup	250 mL	Peanut Butter (smooth or crunchy)
12 oz	365 g	Semisweet Chocolate (for decoration)
4 oz	115 g	Unsweetened Chocolate (for decoration)
1 cup	250 mL	Peanuts chopped medium fine (for decoration)

Preparation:

1. Scald cream in heavy saucepan. Remove from heat and let cool to room temperature. Strain through sieve.
2. Melt chocolate in double boiler over hot water. When melted, remove from heat.
3. Beat butter into chocolate until smooth.
4. Beat in peanut butter until well mixed.
5. Vigorously beat cream into chocolate/peanut butter mixture with whisk until light and fluffy.
6. Chill until firm, approximately 1–3 hours.
7. Scrape spoon or melon-ball cutter across surface of mixture; quickly press with fingertips into 1-inch (2.5 cm) balls. Freeze well wrapped in plastic.

Suggested Decoration:

Dip centers into combination of melted semisweet and unsweetened chocolate to coat. Drop truffles onto a cookie sheet spread with chopped peanuts. Let chocolate set then carefully remove using a spatula if necessary under peanut layer.

Storage:

Store tightly wrapped in plastic in refrigerator for 1 week. Freeze up to 1 month tightly wrapped in plastic.

Notes:

Those famous peanut butter cups take a back seat to this sinfully rich combination!

Hazelnut Truffle

Ingredients:

Yield: 35 – 40

8 oz	250 g	Semisweet Chocolate (chopped into small pieces)
½ cup	125 mL	Whipping Cream
½ cup	125 mL	Chopped, Toasted Hazelnuts
½ cup	125 mL	Hazelnut Nougat or Gianduja Chocolate (if available)
1 cup	250 mL	Finely ground, Toasted Hazelnuts (for decoration)

Preparation:

1. Bring cream just to a boil in a heavy saucepan. Remove from heat.
2. Beat chocolate into cream using hand held mixer or whisk. Beat until smooth and all chocolate is melted.
3. Fold in chopped hazelnuts and mix thoroughly. Chill in refrigerator until firm (1 – 3 hours).
4. If available, cut nougat or Gianduja into ⅜ inch (1 cm) square and press truffle mixture around to form a ball.

   OR

   If Nougat is not available, then form into 1-inch (2.5 cm) balls using spoon or melon-ball cutter. Freeze well wrapped in plastic.

Suggested Decoration:

Roll in chopped hazelnuts to coat evenly.

Storage:

Store in refrigerator well wrapped in plastic for 1 week or freeze in plastic wrap for 1 – 2 months.

Notes:

A hazelnut lovers delight!

Walnut Truffle

Ingredients: Yield: 45 – 50

4 oz	125 g	Milk Chocolate
4 oz	125 g	White Chocolate
2 tbsp	30 mL	Unsalted Butter at room temperature
1 cup	250 mL	Whipping Cream
1 cup	250 mL	Chopped Walnuts
1 lb	500 g	Semisweet Chocolate for decoration
2 cups	500 mL	Walnut Halves (candied if desired) for decoration

Preparation:

1. Scald cream in heavy saucepan. Remove from heat and let cool to room temperature. Strain through sieve.
2. Carefully melt both chocolates together in double boiler over hot water. Remove from heat.
3. With a whisk, beat butter into chocolate until smooth.
4. Vigorously beat cream into chocolate/butter mixture with whisk until light and fluffy.
5. Fold in chopped walnuts mixing well.
6. Chill until firm, approximately 2 – 4 hours.
7. Scrape spoon or melon-ball cutter across surface of mixture; quickly press with fingertips into 1-inch (2.5 cm) balls. Freeze well wrapped in plastic.

Suggested Decoration:

Remove centers from freezer to soften slightly. Press walnut half into top of each truffle and dip in melted chocolate coating only bottom half so walnut is still showing.

Storage:

Store in the refrigerator tightly sealed in plastic for one week. Freeze tightly sealed in plastic for up to one month.

Notes:

This is a difficult decorating treatment but very spectacular.

Macadamia Nut Truffle

Ingredients:

Yield: 45 – 50

8 oz	250 g	White Chocolate
2 tbsp	30 mL	Unsalted Butter (room temperature)
1 cup	250 mL	Whipping Cream
½ cup	125 mL	Unsalted Macadamia nuts finely chopped
1 lb	500 g	White Chocolate (for decoration)
		OR
2 cups	500 g	Chopped, Toasted Macadamia nuts (for decoration)

Preparation:

1. Scald cream in heavy saucepan. Remove from heat and let cool to room temperature. Strain through sieve.
2. Melt chocolate in double boiler over hot water. When melted, remove from heat.
3. Beat butter into chocolate until smooth.
4. Vigorously beat cream into chocolate/butter mixture with whisk until light and fluffy.
5. Fold in Macadamia nuts until well mixed.
6. Chill until firm, approximately 1 – 3 hours.
7. Scrape spoon or melon-ball cutter across surface of mixture; quickly press with fingertips into 1-inch (2.5 cm) balls. Freeze well wrapped in plastic.

Suggested Decoration:

Dip in white chocolate decorating top with white chocolate as desired.

OR

Roll in chopped, toasted Macadamia nuts.

Storage:

Store tightly wrapped in plastic in refrigerator for 1 week. Freeze up to one month tightly wrapped in plastic.

Notes:

This recipe doesn't call for a large quantity of nuts. You can use either of the two suggested decorating ideas depending on your pocketbook!

Almond Bark Truffle

Ingredients:

Yield: 40 – 45

8 oz	250 g	White Chocolate
½ cup	125 mL	Unsalted Butter (room temperature)
¾ cup	175 mL	Slivered Almonds toasted to a golden brown
¾ cup	175 mL	Chopped Toasted Almonds (for decoration)

Preparation:

1. Carefully melt chocolate in a double boiler over hot water. When melted, remove from heat.
2. Vigorously beat butter into warm chocolate with a whisk or at high speed with a hand held mixer until light and fluffy.
3. Fold in slivered almonds until thoroughly mixed.
4. Spoon mixture into a greased 8" x 8" (20 cm x 20 cm) cake pan pressing or tapping on table to level.
5. Sprinkle with chopped almonds, pressing into truffle mixture and coating surface.
6. Chill until firm and cut into 1-inch (2.5 cm) squares.

Storage:

Store tightly wrapped in plastic in refrigerator for 1 week. Freeze up to one month tightly wrapped in plastic.

Notes:

This is a smooth, soft truffle and should be kept refrigerated until serving time.

Pistachio Truffle

Ingredients:

Yield: 42 – 46

8 oz	250 g	White Chocolate
½ cup	125 mL	Unsalted Butter (room temperature)
3	3	Egg yolks at room temperature
½ cup	125 mL	Finely chopped shelled pistachios
¾ cup	175 mL	Finely chopped shelled pistachios (for decoration)

Preparation:

1. Melt chocolate in double boiler over hot water just until melted. Remove from heat.
2. Vigorously beat butter and egg yolks into chocolate.
3. Fold in pistachios, mixing thoroughly.
4. Chill until firm (approximately 1 – 3 hours).
5. Scrape spoon or melon-ball cutter across surface of mixture; quickly press with fingertips into 1-inch (2.5 cm) balls. Freeze well wrapped in plastic.

Suggested Decoration:

Remove truffles a few at a time from the refrigerator and roll in chopped pistachios to coat.

Storage:

The egg yolks make these truffles very perishable. They should be refrigerated until 5 – 10 minutes before serving. They can be frozen for up to one month tightly wrapped in plastic bags.

Notes:

These truffles will be bright green – perfect for the holidays.

Nanaimo Truffle

Ingredients:

Yield: 42 – 45

8 oz	250 g	Semisweet Chocolate (chopped fine)
½ cup	125 mL	Whipping Cream
½ lb	250 g	White Chocolate cut into small pieces approx. ½" x ½" (15 mm x 15 mm)
¼ cup	50 mL	Coconut
¼ cup	50 mL	Graham Crumbs
¼ cup	50 mL	Chopped Walnuts

Preparation:

1. Bring cream just to a boil in a heavy saucepan. Remove from heat.
2. Beat chocolate into cream using hand mixer or whisk. Beat until smooth and all chocolate is melted.
3. Fold in coconut, graham crumbs and walnuts and mix well.
4. Chill mixture for about an hour or until stiff enough to work with.
5. Press chocolate mixture around white chocolate pieces to coat. Try to form an irregular ball. Freeze well wrapped in plastic.

Suggested Decoration:

We think it's great as it is – crumbly and natural looking.

Storage:

Store in refrigerator well wrapped in plastic for 1 week or freeze in plastic wrap for 1 – 2 months.

Notes:

Combine all the ingredients in a Nanaimo bar and what a truffle it makes!

Hazelnut Coffee Truffle

Ingredients:
Yield 45 – 50

4 oz	125 g	Milk Chocolate
4 oz	125 g	White Chocolate
2 tbsp	30 mL	Unsalted Butter (room temperature)
1 cup	250 mL	Whipping Cream
1 tsp	5 mL	Instant Espresso
1 cup	250 mL	Whole Toasted Hazelnuts
1 cup	250 mL	Unsweetened Cocoa

Preparation:
1. Scald cream in heavy saucepan. Remove from heat. Add Instant Espresso to cream and stir until dissolved. Let cool to room temperature and strain through sieve.
2. Carefully melt both chocolates together in double boiler over hot water. Remove from heat.
3. With a whisk, beat butter into chocolate until smooth.
4. Vigorously beat cream into chocolate/butter mixture with whisk until light and fluffy.
5. Chill until firm, approximately 2 – 4 hours.
6. Scrape spoon or melon-ball cutter across surface of mixture; quickly press with fingertips into 1-inch (2.5 cm) balls.
7. Press whole hazelnut into top center of each truffle. Freeze well wrapped in plastic.

Suggested Decoration:
Roll each center in cocoa until coated. Using pastry brush, carefully brush cocoa off hazelnut if possible so it clearly shows through on top.

Storage:
Store in the refrigerator tightly sealed in plastic for one week. Freeze tightly wrapped in plastic for up to one month.

Notes:
Coffee and hazelnut – a wonderful European combination!

Pecan Truffle

Ingredients:
Yield: 40 – 45

4 oz	115 g	Semisweet Chocolate
4 oz	115 g	Milk Chocolate
½ cup	125 mL	Unsalted Butter at room temperature
2 cups	500 g	Whole Pecans preferably large variety, candied, if possible
1 cup	250 mL	Pecan Praline to decorate (optional) See last chapter for instructions

Preparation:

1. Carefully melt chocolate in double boiler over hot water. When melted, remove from heat.
2. Vigorously beat butter into warm chocolate with a whisk or at high speed on a hand held mixer until light and fluffy.
3. Chill mixture until firm, approximately 1 – 3 hours.
4. Scrape spoon or melon-ball cutter across surface of mixture; quickly press with fingertips into 1-inch (2.5 cm) balls.
5. Carefully sandwich the truffle center between two pecan halves. Freeze well wrapped in plastic.

Suggested Decoration:

Dip exposed truffle center between pecans in Praline to coat.

Storage:

Can be kept in the refrigerator well wrapped in plastic for up to 1 month and in the freezer indefinitely.

Notes:

A taste of the old South!

Notes

1. Amaretto Truffle
2. Bourbon Bonbon Truffle
3. Frangelico Truffle
4. Coconut Rum Truffle
5. Kahlua Truffle

Liquor Laced Truffles

Always a historical favorite, the combination of pungent liquor or liqueur with smooth silky chocolate cannot be equaled. The following recipes combine liquor and chocolate in a variety of ways. Please feel free to take poetic licence with each recipe keeping in mind, the ratio of liquor to chocolate. Any liquid, especially liquor, will soften the chocolate mixture. The more liquid added to the ingredients the less likely the mixture will set up properly. Use the recipe as a guide if you want to experiment and have fun. As liquor truffles tend to soften, I have suggested covering them in chocolate in most cases.

Grand Marnier Truffle

Ingredients:

Yield: 30 – 35

8 oz	250 g	Semisweet Chocolate (chopped fine)
½ cup	125 mL	Whipping Cream
⅛ cup	25 mL	Grand Marnier, Triple Sec or Orange Brandy
½ cup	125 mL	Diced Candied Orange Peel (optional)
1 lb	500 g	Semisweet Chocolate for decoration
½ lb	250 g	White Chocolate for decoration

Preparation:

1. Bring Cream just to a boil in heavy saucepan. Remove from heat.
2. Beat chocolate into cream using hand mixer or whisk. Beat until smooth and all chocolate is melted.
3. Beat in liqueur and orange peel until mixture is well blended.
4. Chill in the refrigerator until firm, approximately 1–3 hours.
5. Scrape spoon or melon-ball cutter across surface of mixture; quickly press with fingertips into 1-inch (2.5 cm) balls. Freeze well wrapped in plastic.

Suggested Decoration:

Dip centers in semisweet chocolate and allow to cool completely. Holding dipped centers between thumb and first finger, dip ½ of center in white chocolate; place on parchment paper to cool. Keep hands clean at all times to avoid white fingerprints on dark chocolate half.

Storage:

Store in refrigerator well wrapped in plastic for 1 week or freeze in plastic wrap for 1–2 months.

Notes:

This is our customers' most favorite flavor in truffles. Always a winner with any group.

Amaretto Truffle

Ingredients:

Yield: 40 – 45

4 oz	115 g	Semisweet Chocolate
4 oz	115 g	Milk Chocolate
½ cup	125 mL	Unsalted Butter at room temperature
½ cup	125 mL	Amaretto Liqueur
1 lb	500 g	Semisweet Chocolate for decoration
¼ lb	115 g	Finely chopped toasted almonds for decoration

Preparation:

1. Carefully melt chocolate in double boiler over hot water just until melted. Remove from heat.
2. Vigorously beat butter into warm chocolate with a whisk or at high speed with a hand mixer until light and fluffy.
3. Continue beating and slowly add Amaretto Liqueur.
4. Chill mixture until firm, approximately 1 – 3 hours.
5. Scrape spoon or melon-ball cutter across surface of mixture; quickly press with fingertips into 1-inch (2.5 cm) balls. Freeze well wrapped in plastic.

Suggested Decoration:

Dip centers in melted semisweet chocolate sprinkling chopped almonds on top while chocolate is still wet.

Storage:

Well wrapped in plastic, can be kept in the refrigerator for up to 1 month and in the freezer indefinitely.

Notes:

A favorite with Amaretto lovers!

Kirsch Truffle

Ingredients:

Yield: 40 – 45

8 oz	250 g	White Chocolate
2 tbsp	30 mL	Unsalted Butter at room temperature
1 cup	250 mL	Whipping Cream
1/8 cup	25 mL	Kirsch Liqueur
few drops	few drops	Red food coloring (optional)
1 lb	500 g	Semisweet chocolate for decoration
1/8 lb	55 g	Pink chocolate for decoration

Preparation:

1. Scald cream in heavy saucepan. Remove from heat and let cool to room temperature. Strain through sieve.
2. Melt chocolate in double boiler over hot water. When melted, remove from heat.
3. Beat butter into chocolate until smooth.
4. Beat in Kirsch Liqueur then add just enough red food coloring to tint mixture a light pink. The next step of the addition of cream will lighten mixture even more.
5. Vigorously beat cream into chocolate/butter mixture with whisk until light and fluffy.
6. Chill until firm, approximately 1 – 3 hours.
7. Scrape spoon or melon-ball cutter across surface of mixture; quickly press with fingertips into 1-inch (2.5 cm) balls. Freeze well wrapped in plastic.

Suggested Decoration:

Dip centers in semisweet chocolate and allow to harden. Melt pink coating over low heat, put in a pastry bag and decorate with thin stripes over top of truffles.

Storage:

Store tightly wrapped in plastic in refrigerator for 1 week. Freeze up to one month tightly wrapped in plastic.

Notes:

A beautiful truffle that is a favorite around Valentine's Day.

Crème de Menthe Truffle

Ingredients:

Yield: 25 – 30

2 oz	55 g	Unsweetened Chocolate (chopped fine)
6 oz.	170 g	Semisweet Chocolate (chopped fine)
⅓ cup	75 mL	Crème Fraîche (see last chapter for instructions)
1 tbsp	15 mL	Unsalted Butter (room temperature)
¼ cup	50 mL	Crème de Menthe
1 lb	500 g	Semisweet Chocolate for decoration
¼ lb	115 g	Green Coating for decoration
		OR
½ lb	250 g	Green Coating for decoration
½ lb	250 g	White Coating for decoration
¼ lb	115 g	Dark Chocolate Coating for decoration

Preparation:

1. Bring Crème Fraîche to a boil in heavy saucepan stirring constantly. Remove from heat.
2. Whisk both chocolates into Crème Fraîche until melted and mixture is smooth.
3. Whisk in butter until smooth, and then whisk in Crème de Menthe until smooth.
4. Refrigerate until firm, approximately 1 – 3 hours.
5. Scrape spoon or melon-ball cutter across surface of mixture; quickly press with fingertips into 1-inch (2.5 cm) balls. Freeze well wrapped in plastic.

Suggested Decoration:

Below are two opposite ways of decorating:

1. Dip centers in semisweet chocolate, allow to harden. Using a pastry bag, with green coating, draw stripes on coated truffle.

2. Melt green and white coating together over low heat. Dip centers in coating and allow to harden. Draw stripes on truffles with pastry bag using melted dark coating.

Storage:

Store in the refrigerator well wrapped in plastic for one week. Can be frozen well wrapped in plastic for up to one month.

Notes:

A cool hint of mint adds the finishing touch to this very bittersweet truffle.

Kahlua Truffle

Ingredients:

Yield 35 – 40

8 oz	250 g	Milk Chocolate
½ cup	125 mL	Unsalted Butter (room temperature)
3	3	Egg yolks at room temperature
½ cup	125 mL	Kahlua, Tia Maria or Coffee Liqueur
½ cup	125 mL	Sweetened Cocoa for decoration
½ cup	125 mL	Powdered Coffee for decoration
		OR
1 lb	500 g	Semisweet Chocolate for decoration
		Whole Coffee Beans for decoration

Preparation:

1. Melt chocolate in double boiler over hot water just until melted. Remove from heat.
2. Vigorously beat butter and egg yolks into chocolate.
3. Beat in Coffee Liqueur until well blended.
4. Chill until firm, approximately 1 – 3 hours.
5. Scrape spoon or melon-ball cutter across surface of mixture; quickly press with fingertips into 1-inch (2.5 cm) balls. Freeze well wrapped in plastic.

Suggested Decoration:

Mix cocoa and coffee together until well blended. Roll centers in mixture to coat evenly.

OR

Dip centers in melted semisweet chocolate. Decoratively place 2 coffee beans on top of truffle while chocolate is still wet.

Storage:

Refrigerate well wrapped in plastic for up to one week. They can be frozen well wrapped in plastic for only up to one month.

Notes:

The essence of the Tropics is caught in luscious chocolate. The perfect end to a Latin meal.

Bailey's Cream Truffle

Ingredients:
Yield: 45 – 50

4 oz	125 g	Milk Chocolate
4 oz	125 g	White Chocolate
2 tbsp	30 mL	Unsalted Butter (room temperature)
1 cup	250 mL	Whipping Cream
⅛ cup	25 mL	Irish Whiskey
1 lb	500 g	White Chocolate for decoration
¼ cup	50 mL	Unsweetened Cocoa for decoration
¼ cup	50 mL	Icing Sugar for decoration

Preparation:
1. Scald cream in heavy saucepan. Remove from heat and let cool to room temperature. Strain through sieve.
2. Carefully melt both chocolates together in double boiler over hot water. Remove from heat.
3. With a whisk, beat butter into chocolate until smooth.
4. Stir in Irish whiskey until blended.
5. Vigorously beat cream into chocolate/butter mixture with whisk until light and fluffy.
6. Chill until firm, approximately 2 – 4 hours.
7. Scrape spoon or melon-ball cutter across surface of mixture; quickly press with fingertips into 1-inch (2.5 cm) balls. Freeze well wrapped in plastic.

Suggested Decoration:
Mix cocoa and icing sugar together. Dip centers in white chocolate and sprinkle with cocoa/icing sugar mixture while still wet.

Storage:
Store in the refrigerator tightly sealed in plastic for one week. Freeze tightly sealed in plastic for up to one month.

Notes:
The perfect truffle to celebrate Saint Patrick's Day. Smooth, creamy and very Irish!

Champagne Truffle

Ingredients:

Yield: 35 – 40

8 oz	250 g	Milk Chocolate
½ cup	125 mL	Unsalted Butter at room temperature
3	3	Egg yolks at room temperature
¼ cup	60 mL	Champagne
1 cup	250 g	Icing Sugar (sifted for decoration)

Preparation:

1. Melt chocolate in double boiler over hot water. When melted, remove from heat.
2. Vigorously beat butter and egg yolks into chocolate.
3. Beat in Champagne until well mixed.
4. Chill until firm, approximately 1 – 3 hours.
5. Scrape spoon or melon-ball cutter across surface of mixture; quickly press with fingertips into 1-inch (2.5 cm) balls. Freeze well wrapped in plastic.

Suggested Decoration:

Dip centers in icing sugar to coat. If needed, dip again to get a good white coating.

Storage:

Refrigerate well wrapped in plastic for up to one week. Take out of refrigerator only 5 – 10 minutes before serving. They can be frozen well wrapped in plastic for only up to 1 month.

Notes:

A beautiful truffle with the wonderful, tangy taste of champagne.

Bourbon Bonbon Truffle

Ingredients:

Yield: 45 – 50

4 oz	115 g	Semisweet Chocolate
4 oz	115 g	Milk Chocolate
½ cup	125 mL	Unsalted Butter at room temperature
½ cup	125 mL	Bourbon
1 lb	500 g	Semisweet Chocolate for decoration
¼ cup	50 mL	Unsweetened Cocoa

Preparation:

1. Carefully melt chocolate in double boiler over hot water. When melted, remove from heat.
2. Vigorously beat butter into warm chocolate with a whisk or at high speed with a hand mixer until light and fluffy.
3. Add Bourbon slowly to chocolate mixture as you finish beating it.
4. Chill mixture until firm, approximately 1 – 3 hours.
5. Scrape spoon or melon-ball cutter across surface of mixture; quickly press with fingertips into 1-inch (2.5 cm) balls. Freeze well wrapped in plastic.

Suggested Decoration:

Dip centers in Semisweet chocolate to coat. Since this truffle has no other decoration, the object is to get a perfect bonbon shape to begin with, then coat carefully achieving a smooth surface with no "foot". Dust with cocoa while still wet.

Storage:

Well wrapped in plastic, they can be kept in the refrigerator for up to 1 month and in the freezer indefinitely.

Notes:

That down home Southern favorite combined with smooth chocolate – Heaven y'all!

Calvados Truffle

Ingredients:
Yield: 30–35

8 oz	250 g	Semisweet Chocolate (chopped fine)
½ cup	125 mL	Whipping Cream
⅛ cup	25 mL	Calvados
1 lb	500 g	Semisweet Chocolate for decoration
30–35	30–35	Tiny Chocolate leaves for decoration (see last chapter)

Preparation:
1. Bring Cream just to a boil in a heavy saucepan. Remove from heat.
2. Beat chocolate into Cream using hand mixer or whisk. Beat until smooth and all chocolate is melted.
3. Beat in Calvados until well mixed.
4. Chill in refrigerator until firm, approximately 1–3 hours.
5. Scrape spoon or melon-ball cutter across surface of mixture; quickly press with fingertips into 1-inch (2.5 cm) balls. Freeze well wrapped in plastic.

Suggested Decoration:
Dip centers in Semisweet Chocolate to coat. While still wet, place tiny leaf on top to achieve the look of a small apple.

Storage:
Store in the refrigerator well wrapped in plastic for 1 week or freeze in plastic wrap for 1–2 months.

Notes:
These are elegant truffles that take extra time to decorate but the effect is well worth the effort.

Brandy Truffle

Ingredients:

Yield: 30–35

2 oz	55 g	Unsweetened Chocolate (chopped fine)
6 oz	170 g	Semisweet Chocolate (chopped fine)
⅓ cup	75 mL	Crème Fraîche (see last chapter for instructions)
1 tbsp	15 mL	Unsalted Butter at room temperature
¼ cup	50 mL	Brandy
1 lb	500 g	Dark Vermicelli (chocolate sprinkles) for decoration. (Make sure they are real chocolate)

Preparation:

1. Bring crème fraîche to a boil in heavy saucepan stirring constantly. Remove from heat.
2. Whisk both chocolates into Crème Fraîche until melted and mixture is smooth.
3. Whisk in Brandy to mix well.
4. Whisk in butter until smooth.
5. Refrigerate until firm, approximately 1–3 hours.
6. Scrape spoon or melon-ball cutter across surface of mixture; quickly press with fingertips into 1-inch (2.5 cm) balls.

Suggested Decoration:

Roll centers in Vermicelli to coat. You may find the center mixture needs to be a little soft to coat. I suggest not freezing them before rolling.

Storage:

Store in the refrigerator well wrapped in plastic for one week. Can be frozen well wrapped in plastic for up to one month.

Notes:

The crunchy Vermicelli contrasts nicely with the sharp dark centers.

Pear Brandy Truffle

Ingredients:

Yield: 30 – 35

8 oz	250 g	Semisweet Chocolate (chopped fine)
½ cup	125 mL	Whipping Cream
⅛ cup	25 mL	Pear Brandy
1 cup	250 mL	Unsweetened Cocoa for decoration
30 – 35	30 – 35	Whole Cloves for decoration

Preparation:

1. Bring Cream just to a boil in a heavy saucepan. Remove from heat.
2. Beat chocolate into cream using hand mixer or whisk. Beat until smooth and all chocolate is melted.
3. Beat in Pear Brandy until smooth and well mixed.
4. Chill in refrigerator until firm, approximately 1 – 3 hours.
5. Mold mixture into tiny pear shapes. Push clove into top to represent a pear stem.

Suggested Decoration:

Dust each pear shape carefully in cocoa. Shake off excess.

Storage:

Store in the refrigerator well wrapped in plastic for 1 week or freeze in plastic wrap for 1 – 2 months.

Notes:

Pear Brandy can be very expensive and has a sophisticated taste. To treat the truffle as a work of art may require extra effort but your guests will certainly appreciate it.

Rum Raisin Truffle

Ingredients:

Yield: 40 – 45

4 oz	115 g	Semisweet Chocolate
4 oz	115 g	Milk Chocolate
½ cup	125 mL	Unsalted Butter at room temperature
½ cup	125 mL	Dark Rum
½ cup	125 mL	Raisins, chopped fine
1 lb	500 g	Milk Chocolate for decoration
½ cup	125 mL	Whole Raisins for decoration

Preparation:

1. Soak chopped raisins in rum at least overnight.
2. Carefully melt chocolate in double boiler over hot water. When melted, remove from heat.
3. Vigorously beat butter into warm chocolate with a whisk or at high speed with a hand mixer until light and fluffy.
4. Beat in the raisin/rum combination until chocolate mixture is smooth and well mixed.
5. Chill mixture until firm, approximately 1 – 3 hours.
6. Scrape spoon or melon-ball cutter across surface of mixture; quickly press with fingertips into 1-inch (2.5 cm) balls. Freeze well wrapped in plastic.

Suggested Decoration:

Dip centers in Milk Chocolate, decoratively placing whole raisin on top.

Storage:

Well wrapped in plastic, can be kept in the refrigerator for up to 1 month and in the freezer indefinitely.

Notes:

A rich, wonderful fruit and chocolate combination.

Banana Liqueur Truffle

Ingredients:

Yield: 45 – 50

4 oz	125 g	Milk Chocolate
4 oz	125 g	White Chocolate
2 tbsp	30 mL	Unsalted Butter (room temperature)
1 cup	250 mL	Whipping Cream
1/8 cup	25 mL	Banana Liqueur
1 lb	500 g	Semisweet Chocolate for decoration
1/4 lb	115 g	White Coating for decoration (see last chapter)

Preparation:

1. Scald Cream in heavy saucepan. Remove from heat and let cool to room temperature. Strain through sieve.
2. Carefully melt both chocolates together in double boiler over hot water. Remove from heat.
3. With a whisk, beat butter into chocolate until smooth.
4. Beat in the Banana Liqueur until well mixed.
5. Vigorously beat cream into chocolate mixture with a whisk until light and fluffy.
6. Chill until firm, approximately 2 – 4 hours.
7. Scrape spoon or melon-ball cutter across surface of mixture; quickly press with fingertips into 1-inch (2.5 cm) balls. Freeze well wrapped in plastic.

Suggested Decoration:

Dip centers in semisweet chocolate to coat and set aside to harden. Using a pastry bag, fill with white coating. Draw lines on top of truffle, first in one direction and then in the opposite direction to form a "window pane" design.

Storage:

Store in the refrigerator tightly sealed in plastic for one week. Freeze tightly sealed in plastic for up to one month.

Notes:

Bananas and chocolate – a combination that brings back memories of childhood days of frozen bananas.

Apricot Brandy Truffle

Ingredients:
Yield: 30–35

8 oz	250 g	Semisweet Chocolate (chopped fine)
½ cup	125 mL	Whipping Cream
⅛ cup	25 mL	Apricot Brandy
1 lb	500 g	Semisweet Chocolate for decoration
4 or 5	4 or 5	Dried Apricots sliced into slivers for decoration

Preparation:

1. Bring Cream just to a boil in a heavy saucepan. Remove from heat.
2. Beat chocolate into cream using hand mixer or whisk. Beat until smooth and all chocolate is melted.
3. Beat in Apricot Brandy.
4. Chill until firm, approximately 1–3 hours.
5. Scrape spoon or melon-ball cutter across surface of mixture; quickly press with fingertips into 1-inch (2.5 cm) balls. Freeze well wrapped in plastic.

Suggested Decoration:

Dip centers in Semisweet Chocolate to coat, decoratively placing sliver of apricot on top while chocolate is still wet.

Storage:

Store in refrigerator well wrapped in plastic for 1 week or freeze in plastic for 1–2 months.

Notes:

One of my favorite combinations which adds an elegant touch to winter dinners.

Grand Marnier Cream Truffle

Ingredients:

Yield: 45 – 50

8 oz	250 g	White Chocolate
2 tbsp	30 mL	Unsalted Butter at room temperature
1 cup	250 mL	Whipping Cream
⅛ cup	25 mL	Grand Marnier
few drops	few drops	Orange Food Coloring (optional)
1 lb	500 g	White Chocolate for decoration

Thin slivers of Orange zest curled and candied for decoration.

Preparation:

1. Scald Cream in heavy saucepan. Remove from heat and let it cool to room temperature. Strain through sieve.
2. Melt chocolate in double boiler over hot water. When melted, remove from heat.
3. Beat butter into chocolate until smooth.
4. Vigorously beat cream into chocolate/butter mixture with whisk until light and fluffy.
5. Beat in Grand Marnier then add just enough orange food coloring to tint mixture a light orange color.
6. Chill until firm, approximately 1 – 3 hours.
7. Scrape spoon or melon-ball cutter across surface of mixture; quickly press with fingertips into 1-inch (2.5 cm) balls. Freeze well wrapped in plastic.

Suggested Decoration:

Dip centers in White Chocolate to coat, decoratively placing curled orange zest on top of each while chocolate is still wet.

Storage:

Store tightly wrapped in plastic in the refrigerator for 1 week. Freeze up to one month tightly wrapped in plastic.

Notes:

You'll receive lots of Oohs and Ahhs for these beautiful truffles with a subtle orange taste.

Frangelico Truffle

Ingredients: Yield: 45–50

4 oz	125 g	Milk Chocolate
4 oz	125 g	White Chocolate
2 tbsp	30 mL	Unsalted Butter at room temperature
1 cup	250 mL	Whipping Cream
⅛ cup	25 mL	Frangelico Liqueur
1 lb	500 g	Milk Chocolate for decoration
½ cup	125 mL	Chopped, toasted hazelnuts for decoration

Preparation:

1. Scald Cream in heavy saucepan. Remove from heat and let cool to room temperature. Strain through sieve.
2. Carefully melt both chocolates together in double boiler over hot water. Remove from heat.
3. With a whisk, beat butter into chocolate until smooth.
4. Beat in Frangelico until well mixed.
5. Vigorously beat Cream into chocolate mixture with whisk until light and fluffy.
6. Chill until firm, approximately 2–4 hours.
7. Scrape spoon or melon-ball cutter across surface of mixture; quickly press with fingertips into 1-inch (2.5 cm) balls. Freeze well wrapped in plastic.

Suggested Decoration:

Dip centers in Milk Chocolate to coat completely, sprinkle chopped hazelnuts on top while chocolate is still wet.

Storage:

Store in the refrigerator tightly sealed in plastic for one week. Freeze tightly sealed in plastic for up to one month.

Notes:

A hazelnut lovers delight.

Cherry Marnier Truffle

Ingredients:

Yield: 25 – 30

2 oz	55 g	Unsweetened Chocolate (chopped fine)
6 oz	170 g	Semisweet Chocolate (chopped fine)
⅓ cup	75 mL	Crème Fraîche (see last chapter for instructions)
1 tbsp	15 mL	Unsalted Butter at room temperature
¼ cup	50 mL	Cherry Marnier Liqueur
½ lb	250 g	Semisweet Chocolate shavings for decoration

Preparation:

1. Bring Crème Fraîche to a boil in heavy saucepan stirring constantly. Remove from heat.
2. Whisk both chocolates into Crème Fraîche until melted and mixture is smooth.
3. Whisk in butter until smooth.
4. Whisk in Cherry Marnier until well mixed.
5. Refrigerate until firm, approximately 1 – 3 hours.
6. Scrape spoon or melon-ball cutter across surface of mixture; quickly press with fingertips into 1-inch (2.5 cm) balls.

Suggested Decoration:

Roll soft truffle centers in chocolate shavings to coat completely.

Storage:

Store in the refrigerator well wrapped in plastic for one week. Can be frozen well wrapped in plastic for up to one month.

Notes:

Lovers of Black Forest Cakes will be ecstatic over this truffle.

Amaretto Cream Truffle

Ingredients:
Yield: 45 – 50

8 oz	250 g	White Chocolate
2 tbsp	30 mL	Unsalted Butter at room temperature
1 cup	250 mL	Whipping Cream
⅛ cup	25 mL	Amaretto Liqueur
½ cup	125 mL	Chopped, toasted Almonds
¾ cup	175 mL	Icing Sugar for decoration
¼ cup	50 mL	Unsweetened Cocoa for decoration

Preparation:
1. Scald cream in heavy saucepan. Remove from heat and let cool to room temperature. Strain through sieve.
2. Melt chocolate in double boiler over hot water. When melted, remove from heat.
3. Beat butter into chocolate until smooth.
4. Beat Amaretto Liqueur and almonds into chocolate mixture until well mixed.
5. Vigorously beat cream into chocolate mixture with whisk until light and fluffy.
6. Chill until firm, approximately 1 – 3 hours.
7. Scrape spoon or melon-ball cutter across surface of mixture; quickly press with fingertips into 1-inch (2.5 cm) balls. Freeze well wrapped in plastic.

Suggested Decoration:
Combine icing sugar and cocoa and sift into shallow dish. Roll centers in mixture to coat evenly.

Storage:
Store tightly wrapped in plastic in refrigerator for 1 week. Freeze well wrapped in plastic for up to one month.

Notes:
A sweet, nutty truffle that is perfect for afternoon tea.

Coconut Rum Truffle

Ingredients:

Yield: 40 – 45

8 oz	250 g	White Chocolate
2 tbsp	30 mL	Unsalted Butter (room temperature)
1 cup	250 mL	Whipping Cream
¼ cup	50mL	Coconut Liqueur
¼ cup	50mL	White Rum
		OR
¼ cup	50 mL	Coconut Rum Liqueur
1 lb	500 g	Semisweet Chocolate for decoration
½ cup	125 mL	Shreaded Coconut for decoration

Preparation:

1. Scald cream in heavy saucepan. Remove from heat and let cool to room temperature. Strain through sieve.
2. Melt chocolate in double boiler over hot water. When melted, remove from heat.
3. Beat butter into chocolate until smooth.
4. Beat in coconut rum liqueur and white rum OR coconut rum liqueur until well blended.
5. Vigorously beat cream into chocolate mixture with whisk until light and fluffy.
6. Chill until firm, approximately 1 – 3 hours.
7. Scrape spoon or melon-ball cutter across surface of mixture; quickly press with fingertips into 1-inch (2.5 cm) balls. Freeze well wrapped in plastic.

Suggested Decoration:

Dip centers in semisweet chocolate and sprinkle coconut on top while chocolate is still wet.

Storage:

Store tightly wrapped in plastic in refrigerator for 1 week. Freeze up to one month tightly wrapped in plastic.

Notes:

A beautiful white and dark truffle with a real punch!

Chestnut Liqueur Truffle

Ingredients:
Yield: 35 – 40

8 oz	250 g	Milk Chocolate
½ cup	125 mL	Unsalted Butter at room temperature
3	3	Egg yolks at room temperature
½ cup	125 mL	Chestnut Liqueur
1 lb	500 g	White Chocolate for decoration
½ lb	250 g	Milk Chocolate Coating for decoration

Preparation:
1. Melt chocolate in double boiler over hot water just until melted. Remove from heat.
2. Vigorously beat butter and egg yolks into chocolate.
3. Beat in Chestnut Liqueur until well blended.
4. Chill until firm, approximately 1 – 3 hours.
5. Scrape spoon or melon-ball cutter across surface of mixture; quickly press with fingertips into 1-inch (2.5 cm) balls. Freeze well wrapped in plastic.

Suggested Decoration:
Dip centers into white chocolate to coat completely and let harden. Dip ½ of each truffle into milk chocolate to coat.

Storage:
Refrigerate well wrapped in plastic for up to one week. Take out of refrigerator only 5 – 10 minutes before serving. They can be frozen well wrapped in plastic for only up to one month.

Notes:
Holiday time and the spirit of Chestnuts go wonderfully together.

Praline Liqueur Truffle

Ingredients:
Yield: 35–40

8 oz	250 g	Milk Chocolate
½ cup	125 mL	Unsalted Butter at room temperature
3	3	Egg yolks at room temperature
½ cup	125 mL	Praline Liqueur
1 cup	250 mL	Chopped Praline for decoration

Preparation:
1. Melt chocolate in double boiler over hot water just until melted. Remove from heat.
2. Vigorously beat butter and egg yolks into chocolate.
3. Beat in Praline Liqueur until well blended.
4. Chill until firm, approximately 1–3 hours.
5. Scrape spoon or melon-ball cutter across surface of mixture; quickly press with fingertips into 1-inch (2.5 cm) balls.

Suggested Decoration:
While centers are soft, roll them into chopped Praline to coat completely.

Storage:
As the Praline coating will go sticky if exposed to air, it is best to store these truffles in an air tight container in the refrigerator or at room temperature. Remember, however, that the egg yolks make these quite perishable, and they cannot be kept for longer than a week.

Notes:
The spirit of New Orleans – Smooth with a hint of excitement!

Notes

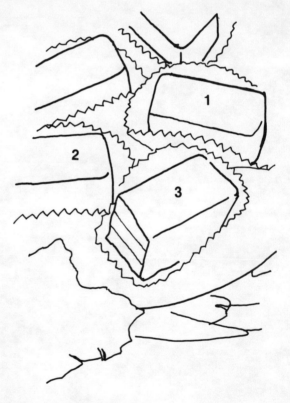

1. B52 Truffle
2. Caramel Pear Truffle
3. Black Russian Truffle

"Combinations Made in Heaven"

Our famous B52 Truffle was the start of a whole new look at Truffles. The beautiful layers blend together on the tongue to make a wonderful different flavor. Because of the bar or square shape, a complete coating of chocolate with a simple design is all that is needed for presentation.

B52 Truffle

Ingredients:

Yield: 25 – 35

1	1	Recipe Bailey's Cream Truffle (Page 89)
½	½	Recipe Kahlua Truffle (Page 88)
½	½	Recipe Grand Marnier Truffle (Page 84)
2 lbs	1000 g	Semisweet Chocolate for decoration
¼ lb	115 g	White Coating for decoration

Preparation:

1. Make Bailey's Cream Truffle recipe. Pour into an 8" x 8" (20 x 20 cm) square pan, lined with parchment. Tap on counter to level and place in the refrigerator to chill.
2. Make Kahlua Truffle recipe. Pour over Bailey's Cream layer. Tap on counter to level and place in the refrigerator to chill.
3. Make Grand Marnier Truffle recipe. Pour over Kahlua Truffle layer. Tap on counter to level and place in freezer to chill completely.
4. Cut into 1" x 1" (2.5 x 2.5 cm) or 1" x 1½" (2.5 x 4 cm) bars. Freeze well wrapped in plastic.

Suggested Decoration:

Dip each bar or square in Semisweet Chocolate to coat completely and let harden. Using a pastry bag, with white coating, write B52 on top of each.

Storage:

Store in refrigerator well wrapped in plastic for 1 week or freeze in plastic wrap for 1 – 2 months.

Notes:

You'll find the truffle mixture hard to cut unless it is frozen. Keep bars or squares frozen while you are dipping. They become very soft at room temperature.

Hazelnut Praline Truffle

Ingredients:

Yield: 30–35

1	1	Hazelnut Truffle recipe (Page 71)
1	1	Praline Liqueur Truffle recipe (Page 104)
½ cup	125 mL	Chopped, toasted Hazelnuts
2 lbs	1000 g	Milk Chocolate for decoration

Preparation:

1. Make Hazelnut Truffle recipe and pour into an 8" x 8" (20 x 20 cm) pan lined with parchment paper. Tap to level. Sprinkle chopped hazelnuts over Hazelnut Truffle layer saving ⅛ cup (25 mL) for decoration. Press nuts into truffle layer. Put in fridge to chill.

2. Make Praline Truffle recipe. Pour over Hazelnut layer and tap gently to level. Place in freezer to chill completely.

3. Cut into squares 1" x 1" (2.5 x 2.5 cm) or into bars 1" x 1½" (2.5 x 4 cm). Place in freezer well wrapped in plastic.

Suggested Decoration:

Dip squares or bars in Milk Chocolate to coat completely. Sprinkle reserved hazelnuts on top while chocolate is still wet.

Storage:

Store in the refrigerator well wrapped in plastic for up to one week. Can be frozen well wrapped in plastic for 1–2 months.

Notes:

Hazelnuts – smooth, crunchy and with a delightful liqueur flavor.

Espresso Bean/ Kahlua Truffle

Ingredients:

Yield: 30 – 35

1	1	Espresso Truffle Recipe (Page 40)
1	1	Kahlua Truffle Recipe (Page 88)
2 lbs	1000 g	Semisweet Chocolate for decoration
		Espresso Beans for decoration

Preparation:

1. Make Espresso Truffle recipe. Pour into 8" x 8" (20 x 20 cm) pan lined with parchment paper. Tap on counter to level. Place in refrigerator to chill.

2. Make Kahlua Truffle recipe and pour over Espresso layer. Tap gently to level and place in freezer to chill completely.

3. Cut into bars 1" x 1½" (2.5 x 4 cm) or squares 1" x 1" (2.5 x 2.5 cm). Store in the freezer well wrapped in plastic.

Suggested Decoration:

Dip squares or bars in Semisweet Chocolate to coat completely. Place 1 espresso bean in a corner of coated square or bar while chocolate is still wet.

Storage:

Store in the refrigerator well wrapped in plastic for several weeks or freeze well wrapped in plastic for 1 month.

Notes:

The Espressoholics delight!!

Apricot Sacher Truffle

Ingredients:

Yield: 30 – 35

1	1	Very Bittersweet Chocolate Truffle recipe (Page 28)
1	1	Apricot Brandy Truffle recipe (Page 97)
½ cup	125 mL	Dried Apricots, chopped
2 lbs	1000 g	Semisweet Chocolate

Preparation:

1. Make Very Bittersweet Chocolate Truffle recipe. Pour into an 8" x 8" (20 x 20 cm) pan lined with parchment paper. Tap on counter to level. Sprinkle with chopped apricots reserving ⅛ cup (25 mL) for decoration. Press chopped apricots into truffle mixture and place in the refrigerator to chill.

2. Make Apricot Brandy Truffle recipe. Pour over Very Bittersweet layer. Tap gently on counter to level and place in freezer to chill completely.

3. Cut into 1" x 1" (2.5 x 2.5 cm) squares or 1" x 1½" (2.5 x 4 cm) bars. Place in freezer tightly wrapped in plastic.

Suggested Decoration:

Dip in Semisweet Chocolate to coat completely. Decorate with apricot piece while chocolate is still wet.

Storage:

Store in the refrigerator tightly wrapped in plastic for several weeks or store in the freezer tightly wrapped in plastic for a month.

Notes:

Deep, very dark, sinfully rich Truffle!

Florentine Truffle

Ingredients:

Yield: 30 – 35

½	½	Recipe for Orange Truffle (Page 42)
1	1	Recipe for Amaretto Cream Truffle (Page 101)
½	½	Recipe for Vanilla Truffle (Page 47)
2 lbs	1000 g	Semisweet Chocolate for decoration
		Sliced, toasted Almonds for decoration

Preparation:

1. Make Orange Truffle recipe. Pour into an 8" x 8" (20 x 20 cm) pan lined with parchment paper. Tap on counter to level. Place in refrigerator to chill.
2. Make Amaretto Cream Truffle recipe. Pour over Orange layer. Tap gently to level. Place in the refrigerator to chill.
3. Make Vanilla Truffle recipe. Pour over Amaretto Cream layer. Tap gently to level. Put in freezer to chill completely.
4. Cut into 1" x 1" (2.5 x 2.5 cm) squares or 1" x 1½" (2.5 x 4 cm) bars. Place in the freezer tightly wrapped in plastic.

Suggested Decoration:

Dip in Semisweet Chocolate to coat completely. Decorate with almond slice while chocolate is still wet.

Storage:

Store in the refrigerator tightly wrapped in plastic for several weeks or store in the freezer tightly wrapped in plastic for a month.

Notes:

A wonderful combination reminiscent of the florentine cookie.

Nutty Irishman Truffle

Ingredients:

Yield: 30 – 35

1	1	Recipe Bailey's Cream Truffle (Page 89)
1	1	Recipe Frangelico Truffle (Page 99)
1 lb	500 g	White Chocolate for decoration
1 lb	500 g	Milk Chocolate for decoration

Preparation:

1. Make Bailey's Cream Truffle recipe. Pour into an 8" x 8" (20 x 20 cm) pan lined with parchment paper. Tap on counter to level. Place in refrigerator to chill.

2. Make Frangelico Truffle recipe. Pour over the Bailey's layer. Tap gently to level. Place in the freezer to chill completely.

3. Cut into 1" x 1" (2.5 x 2.5 cm) squares or 1" x 1½" (2.5 x 4 cm) bars. Place in freezer tightly wrapped in plastic.

Suggested Decoration:

Dip one-half bar or square into white chocolate on the diagonal. Let harden in freezer. Dip remaining half into Milk Chocolate coating slightly over white chocolate layer to seal.

Storage:

Store in the refrigerator tightly wrapped in plastic for several weeks or in the freezer tightly wrapped in plastic for a month.

Notes:

Decorating these can be a little tricky but the result is well worth it both in presentation and taste.

Caramel Pear Truffle

Ingredients:

Yield: 30–35

1	1	Recipe Caramel Truffle (Page 45)
1	1	Recipe Pear Brandy Truffle (Page 94)
2 lbs	1000 g	Semisweet Chocolate for decoration
¼ lb	125 g	White Coating for decoration

Preparation:

1. Make Caramel Truffle recipe and pour into an 8" x 8" (20 x 20 cm) pan lined with parchment paper. Tap lightly to level. Place in the refrigerator to chill.

2. Make Pear Brandy recipe. Pour over Caramel Truffle layer. Tap gently to level. Place in the freezer to chill completely.

3. Cut into 1" x 1" (2.5 x 2.5 cm) squares or 1" x 1½" (2.5 x 4 cm) bars. Place in the freezer tightly wrapped in plastic.

Suggested Decoration:

Dip in Semisweet Chocolate coating completely. Using a pastry bag, pipe a decoration across top of truffle using white chocolate coating.

Storage:

Store in the refrigerator tightly wrapped in plastic for several weeks or store in the freezer tightly wrapped in plastic for a month.

Notes:

Reminiscent of poached pears with caramel sauce.

Tangerine Truffle

Ingredients:

Yield: 30 – 35

1	1	Recipe Grand Marnier Truffle (Page 84)
1	1	Recipe Grand Marnier Cream Truffle (Page 98)
1	1	Large can Tangerine Sections drained for decoration or fresh tangerine sections (approximately 5 tangerines or mandarin oranges)
2 lbs	1000 g	Semisweet Chocolate for decoration

Preparation:

1. Make Grand Marnier Truffle recipe. Pour into an 8" x 8" (20 x 20 cm) pan, lined with parchment paper. Tap to level. Place in the refrigerator to chill.

2. Make Grand Marnier Cream Truffle recipe. Pour over Grand Marnier layer. Tap gently to level. Place in the freezer to chill completely.

3. Cut into 1" x 1" (2.5 x 2.5 cm) squares or 1" x 1½" (2.5 x 4 cm) bars. Place in the freezer tightly wrapped in plastic.

Suggested Decoration:

Dip in Semisweet Chocolate to coat completely. Place a tangerine slice on one corner of truffle while chocolate is still wet.

Storage:

Store in the refrigerator tightly wrapped in plastic for a week. Store in the freezer tightly wrapped in plastic for a month.

Notes:

A gorgeous truffle that should be decorated only a day before serving as the tangerine slice will dry out.

Black Russian Truffle

Ingredients:

Yield: 30 – 35

1	1	Recipe Kahlua Truffle (Page 88)
½	½	Recipe Espresso Truffle without Espresso Beans (Page 40)
½	½	Recipe White Chocolate Truffle (Page 33)
2 lbs	1000 g	Semisweet Chocolate for decoration
¼ cup	50 mL	White Coating for decoration

Preparation:

1. Make Kahlua Truffle recipe. Pour into 8" x 8" (20 x 20 cm) pan lined with parchment paper. Tap to level. Place in the refrigerator to chill.
2. Make Espresso Truffle recipe. Pour over Kahlua layer. Tap gently to level. Place in the refrigerator to chill.
3. Make White Chocolate Truffle recipe. Pour over Espresso layer. Tap to level. Chill in the freezer.
4. Cut into 1" x 1" (2.5 x 2.5 cm) squares or 1" x 1½" (2.5 x 4 cm) bars. Place in the freezer tightly wrapped in plastic.

Suggested Decoration:

Dip into Semisweet Chocolate to coat completely. Let harden. Using Pastry bag, pipe white coating across top of truffle in diagonal stripes.

Storage:

Store in the refrigerator tightly wrapped in plastic for several weeks or store in the freezer tightly wrapped in plastic for a month.

Notes:

A deep, rich coffee taste that is mellowed by the addition of a sweet white chocolate layer.

Notes

Notes

Presentation – That Essential Ingredient

One of the most important aspects in the preparation of fine food is the final presentation. In this chapter I will discuss all the various ways of decorating Truffles in order to make their final presentation beautiful and mouth watering.

Index

Working with Fine Chocolate

As I discuss working with fine chocolate, I am referring to real chocolate containing only cocoa butter as the oil. I will discuss non-real chocolate, those compounds containing vegetable oil in place of cocoa butter in the next section.

Real chocolate is an emulsion of Cocoa solids (powder), Cocoa butter and sugar. Dry milk powder, lecithin and vanilla can also be added to produce different flavors.

The quality of the chocolate depends entirely on the quality of the original ingredients. Chocolate manufacturers produce a wide range of qualities from fabulous to poor, in order to supply the differing demands of the marketplace. The finest cocoa beans blended specifically for luxury chocolate coupled with added cocoa butter produce a wonderful high quality product. For the home Truffle maker, finding a top quality chocolate or Couverture (chocolate especially formulated usually with a higher cocoa butter content for the food industry) can be almost impossible. The most important things to do in looking for real chocolate are to taste the product and to read the label. In this case, less rather than more ingredients are important. A beautiful chocolate contains only cocoa (also known as chocolate liquor or chocolate solids), Cocoa Butter and Sugar in that order. A lack of Cocoa Butter means it cannot be real chocolate. Also, if sugar comes first on the listing, it gives you an indication of the sweetness of the product. Make sure you taste and compare before you use a particular chocolate. The smoother, less sweet, melt in your mouth properties are very important in a truffle or any chocolate confection. Let your taste buds be the final judge.

Now that you've found the best chocolate available, you have to learn to work with it. Only Confectioners coating (chocolate without cocoa butter) can be used for dipping and molding by just melting. Real chocolate that contains large amounts of cocoa butter must be "tempered" after melting and before using. The finer the chocolate, the higher the proportion of cocoa butter and the more important the tempering process becomes. If real chocolate is not tempered before using, the cocoa butter will not emulsify with other ingredients resulting in white streaks and a melting consistency. The instructions for tempering follow and should be used for all flavors of real chocolate.

Chocolate Dipping and Tempering

Equipment needed:

1 lb	500 g	Pure chocolate broken into pieces
4 oz	115 g	Pure chocolate grated as finely as possible

Double boiler • Wooden spoon • Candy thermometer

Cold tap water in bowl or pan approximately same size as double boiler bottom

Steps in tempering:

1. Place 1 lb (500 g) chocolate into double boiler over hot water. Be careful to stir and watch that water doesn't boil. Insert candy thermometer into chocolate mass and monitor the temperature constantly.

2. When temperature reaches 100°F (34°C) remove top of double boiler and place in cold water bath, continuing to stir vigorously as temperature drops. Add grated chocolate by tablespoons. After every two tablespoon additions, beat until shavings are dissolved.

3. When temperature reaches 87°F (30°C) remove a small amount of chocolate from double boiler and spread on marble slab or cooled plate. Let this amount harden to test that remaining chocolate is tempered.

4. As the test batch is hardening, make sure to maintain a temperature of 87°F (30°C) and continue stirring. Don't forget around sides and bottom of the pan, as these areas cool faster.

5. If test is positive – in that the chocolate remains smooth and glossy, it is ready to be used for molding and dipping. If there are any grey streaks or dull areas, return test chocolate to the double boiler and repeat tempering process from step #1.

6. Dipping centers – drop center into chocolate. Using dipping or dinner fork, retrieve center by lifting gently out of chocolate. Lightly tap fork on side of pan to remove excess chocolate. (This prevents a pool of excess chocolate on bottom of finished chocolate called a "foot"). Carefully place chocolate on parchment or wax paper lined tray to harden. You can also use your fingers for dipping. Release truffle from fingertips onto parchment swirling top for a decorative finish.

Uses of Confectioners Coating

Confectioners coating is an emulsion of cocoa powder, vegetable oil (such as palm oil or coconut oil), sugar and possibly dry milk powder. It comes in a variety of flavors and as it contains no cocoa butter, it does not have to be tempered before using. It comes in chocolate flavors of dark and milk chocolate as well as non chocolate colors of pink, green, white and yellow. These colored confections are made to resemble white chocolate in flavor and are an emulsion of vegetable oil, sugar, and dry milk powder.

These chocolate or colored wafers can be used for decorating dipped truffles as they impart very little flavor and do not have to be tempered before using.

Make a pastry bag out of parchment by cutting the parchment into a triangle and then forming it into a cone. Seal the edge by stapling or taping. Fill the cone with warm melted coating. Fold up the end and snip off the tip. You now have a small pastry bag shape full of coating that can be kept warm for use during the time that you are working with it. The easiest way to keep the bag warm is by placing it on the warm surface of the stove.

Use the tip like a pen to draw lines, initials etc. on the top of the truffles. You can also draw designs on a piece of parchment, let them cool and place on the truffle. Our Calvados truffle has a small leaf that is drawn separately on parchment, allowed to harden, then placed on the top of the wet truffle to resemble an apple leaf.

Cocoa and Icing (Confectioners) Sugar Coatings for Truffles

Unsweetened or sweetened cocoa can be used as a coating for truffles. This is the classic French way to present truffles. It is recommended to roll centers in cocoa once, let dry, and then roll again. The cocoa acts as a sealer around center and prevents the center from drying out.

Icing or confectioners sugar can be used in the same manner as cocoa. You may find on a very liqueur infused center, a third rolling in the sugar might be necessary.

A combination of icing sugar and cocoa makes a third coating medium. The proportion of sugar to cocoa can vary according to the result you desire. From a slightly pink coating to a rich cocoa brown coating.

Colored Sugar

Colored sugars make an interesting if very sweet coating on truffle centers. You can usually purchase large colored crystals at the supermarket. I prefer to color my own berry (or super fine) granulated sugar. The coating will then be lighter as the crystals are smaller.

To make colored sugar you will need paste food color rather than liquid food color. The easiest way is to put a quantity of sugar in your food processor or blender. Add a tiny amount of paste color and blend until color is distributed evenly. I usually do this by hand since I'm only doing a small amount at a time. Place sugar and color in a small bowl and rub color into sugar with spoon or pestle. It takes longer but the clean up is easy when only a small amount is needed.

Candied Fruit Peel

2 cups	500 mL	Water
2½ cups	625 mL	Sugar
2 or 3	2 or 3	Oranges, Grapefruits or Lemons

Peel skin from fruit very carefully so no white pith is attached to peel. To remove the bitterness from the peel, blanch it in boiling water for 5 minutes. Remove peel from water and refresh it by running it under cold water. Blanch once again for 5 minutes in fresh boiling water, and again refresh it by running it under cold water. Drain peel on paper towels.

Put sugar and water in heavy saucepan and bring to a boil stirring constantly until all sugar is dissolved. Add the drained peel and cook over low heat for 3 hours. Syrup should barely simmer.

Remove Peel from syrup and place on wire rack to drain. Store in airtight container.

Caramel Sprinkles

| ⅔ cup | 150 mL | Water |
| 2 cups | 500 mL | Sugar |

Bring sugar and water to a boil stirring constantly until all sugar is dissolved. Stop stirring and continue cooking until syrup reaches light caramel stage 320°–330°F (160°–165°C). Immediately pour onto parchment paper in thin layer. Let Caramel cool. Break and chop into small sprinkles. Store in airtight container. The sprinkles tend to get sticky at room temperature when out of storage. Truffles that have been rolled in caramel sprinkles should be served immediately.

Praline (Nut Brittle)

1 cup	250 g	Nuts blanched, toasted and still warm (preferably Pecans or Hazelnuts)
2/3 cup	150 mL	Water
2 cups	500 mL	Sugar

Bring sugar and water to a boil stirring constantly to dissolve all sugar. Brush down sugar crystals from around edge of pan during this time. When syrup boils stop stirring and boil until temperature reaches 320°–330°F (160°–165°C). Syrup will be a light caramel color. Immediately remove from heat and put bottom of pan in cold water to stop cooking. Add warm nuts shaking pan to mix quickly. Pour nuts and syrup onto parchment paper or oiled counter, spreading quickly with a spatula to make a thin layer.

When brittle has cooled, it can be broken into pieces and chopped finely for praline. Store in an airtight container immediately as the praline tends to get sticky if left at room temperature.

Crispy Meringue

| 4 | 4 | Egg whites |
| 1 cup | 250 mL | Sugar |

Place egg whites and sugar in top of double boiler and beat with whisk until mixture feels warm and sugar is dissolved. Remove from heat and continue beating with electric mixer at high speed for 5 minutes. Then lower speed to medium and beat until meringue forms very stiff peaks. Spread a thin layer on a parchment lined cookie sheet.

Bake at 275°F (135°C) for 40 to 50 minutes, leaving oven door ajar with a stick. Reduce heat to warm and continue drying meringue until crisp throughout. You can turn off the oven and leave the meringue overnight to dry. Chop into small chunks and store in an airtight container.

Crème Fraîche

Ingredients:

Yield: 1 cup (250 mL)

| 1 cup | 250 mL | Whipping Cream |
| 2 tbsp | 30 mL | Buttermilk |

Preparation:

1. Heat cream and buttermilk in a heavy saucepan until just warm to the touch.
2. Let stand in a warm place (on top of the fridge or stove) approximately 8 hours or overnight.
3. When crème has formed thick layer on top with a liquid layer underneath it is ready.
4. Place in covered container, stir to mix, and store in refrigerator overnight before using.

Storage:

Crème Fraîche will keep up to one week when it is kept under refrigeration.

Chocolate Storage and Handling Tips

1. Store chocolate in a cool place, approximately 65°F (18°C) but not in the refrigerator, as any moisture will alter the chocolate's appearance.

2. A "bloom" will develop on chocolate that has been exposed to high temperatures. This doesn't affect the flavor or freshness, but gives the chocolate a grey cast which is the cocoa butter rising to the surface.

3. Be careful not to drop water into your chocolate unless the recipe specifies it. The water will change the consistency of the chocolate, causing it to tighten or harden.

4. Don't cover melting chocolate with a lid as the steam will collect and fall as water droplets. Use a light cloth cover if needed.

5. Use low heat when melting chocolate. Chocolate scorches easily and becomes a grainy mass unsuitable for use.

6. Use coconut oil, vegetable oil or shortening, not butter as a thinning agent. These oils are similar to cocoa butter.

7. Chocolate will continue to melt even after it is removed from a heat source. Care in heating is needed as the temperature will rise well after removal from heat source.

8. Unsweetened chocolate will liquefy when melted. Sweetened chocolate will hold its shape until it is stirred.

9. Chocolate flavored coating is used for glazing, dipping, and molding as it needs no tempering. Coating contains cocoa plus a vegetable oil instead of cocoa butter. The quality is not as high as real chocolate but coatings are popular because they are easier to use.

10. Chocolate is very sensitive to odors. Be careful when storing near other foods. Also make sure all utensils are clean and odorless.

11. When blending chocolate flavors, make sure and use the same brand. Different companies put different ingredients into their chocolate which may not mix smoothly.

Index

Index